25/3

The Wakhan Corridor

by

Lawrence Bransby

Copyright © Lawrence Bransby 2015
Lawrence Bransby has asserted his right to be identified as the Author of this work in accordance with the Copyright, Designs and Patent Act, 1988. All rights reserved. No part of this publication may be reproduced or transmitted in any form or by any means, electronic or mechanical, including photocopy, recording, or any information storage and retrieval system, without permission in writing from the copyright owner.
Cover design by Clive Thompson (cliveleet@mweb.co.za)

ISBN 9781521800027

Please note: I have published this book without photographs to lower the purchase price. As we live in the digital world, I encourage you to go to www.hareti.co.uk, my son's website, where you will be able to see a large selection of photographs and some video footage taken during the journey described here as well as the GPS download of our route. (The e-book, however, has been published with photographs.)

"One has to leave the world to discover it."

Thomas Merton, Trappist monk.

"Motorbikes impose the uniqueness of places on their occupants. They eliminate the option to be ignorant of circumstance. The perilous complexity of riding focuses the mind and grants a reprieve from mundane worries."

Jonathan Mummolo

It was me who done it

OK, it was me who done it.

I'd rather make a clean breast of it right at the start so no one can accuse me of prevarication: I was the one who suggested we stop for lunch that day.

There, I've admitted it.

It was me.

And it wasn't as if it was a decent lunch anyway - some nondescript soup with a piece of gristly bone in it, a large hunk of potato and carrot floating in some watery stuff.

And dry bread. Always dry bread.

And it was that lunch stop that changed the entire journey.

If we hadn't paused, rested a little, lingered over our gristly piece of bone, we would have made it over the pass before the landslide deposited half a mountain onto the road and blocked it for the next ten days.

We would have been blissfully riding along the Pamir Highway, singing joyfully into our helmets without a care in the world. All would have gone according to plan...

But, then - maybe not.

Maybe we would have been *in* the cutting when the rocks came roaring down.

Then we would have been dead and, logically, you wouldn't be reading this.

And, as we rode the six hard days to get round the rock fall, many times I thought about that seemingly inconsequential decision that set off a concatenation of events that rewrote the story of our journey.

Had we not stopped for that mediocre bite to eat, we would have met entirely different people, experienced dissimilar things, maybe ridden over a cliff (instead of *nearly* riding over a cliff) or had a sudden, unplanned altercation with a truck around a tight corner.

Who knows?

During the long hours of riding I came to realise how every moment of our lives dictates a different future (sorry - riding long distances makes me deeply and profoundly philosophical, a bit like a drunk man solving the problems of the world). Mundane decisions like: *Do I need a pee now or can I wait until we next stop?* begin us on a completely new trajectory in life. Stop for a pee now and forty seven minutes later run over the Danish woman you end up marrying; suffer for another hour and meet an entirely different woman whom you follow to Australia.

It reminds me of that film *Sliding Doors* - the butterfly effect of just making it through a sliding door or not, a matter of *one second*, and how that miniscule hiccough of time, that seemingly inconsequential hesitation can profoundly affect the rest of your life. (Like those people who, on that fateful day, didn't go into the World Trade Centre, maybe because someone casually said, "Hey, let's stop for a quick bite to eat...")

And, so, this is the version of the story of a brief slice of my life during which my son, Gareth, and I travelled along the Palmir Highway and alongside the Wakhan Corridor in Central Asia, the slice dictated by my decision to stop for a mediocre bite to eat.

If I hadn't suggested we stop, you'd be reading an entirely different story.

Or maybe not reading one at all...

Why the 'Stans?

So, a motorcycle trip to the 'Stans. Why did we favour this particular, rather remote part of the world over any other?

It happened like this:

After our last trip - to Morocco - Gareth sent me an email with a link to www.englishrussia.com and a richly illustrated article called "Landscapes of Kirghizia". His typically terse message was just two words long:

"Next year?"

And immediately the feelings of wanderlust began to play about in my mind. I emailed him a tentative: *Are you serious about this?* but was sad when he replied that, no, it's just too far away.

Just a dream.

Just a maybe...

But I kept the link and was drawn to it again and again, like a child to sweets kept just out of reach on a high shelf and, because seemingly unobtainable, even more desirable.

Then, a few months later, Gareth phoned me: An Iranian friend was looking for a passenger to help pay petrol costs when he drove his camper van from the UK back to Iran. Did he have any suggestions?

Gareth didn't quite say, "Is the Pope a Catholic?" but said he knew of someone who would jump at the chance and, naturally, he phoned me.

"I'm in!" I told him without taking a breath.

But then, thinking about it more rationally, I had doubts. Driving all the way from England to Iran in a camper van with two strangers and then making my way home by train and air didn't quite grab me.

Then came the thought: What if I paid him a little more and we took my bike to Iran with us on a trailer and then I could ride back?

Now we were talking! Yes, I could do this.

But then, when I looked at distances, it seemed just too far for me to do in a month - the time I felt was justified to take off on a bike trip, leaving my wife alone at home.

Still, the idea of Iran piqued my interest. What if, I put to Gareth, we fly the bikes to Theran and ride them back? How about that?

The next day he emailed me with a link to Google Maps headed:

"Trip".

(Gareth, like Twitter, thinks that he only has a limited number of words he can use each day so he rations them.) His message above the Google Maps link said: *"Then back home through Kazakhstan and Russia."*

No, "Hi, Dad - I was just thinking..."

Where bike trips are concerned, we don't need to communicate like that. His fingers, like mine, tremble over small tracks on a map, caressing the surface with slightly unfocussed eyes, planning, imagining...

I opened the Google Maps link to see the dark blue line of a tentative route beginning at Tabriz in Iran, then to Hehran, Mashhd, across the Uzbekistan border to Samarkand, into Tajikistan to Dushanbe, across the Kyrgystan border to Bishkek "...then back home through Kazakhstan and Russia".

Kyrgyzstan...   Uzbekistan...   Tajikistan...   Kazakhstan... Turkmenistan...

The words roll off the tongue with a raw sensuousness.

Well, they do for me.

The *remoteness* of them, the foreignness of their cluttered syllables, produces a warm tightening in the belly, a heightened pulse rate, and evokes a restless desire in the spirit that makes me want to head out into the world and do brave and gallant things. Like when you open a map of a country you haven't explored before and skim your eyes over its surface, seeking out the empty spaces, the *Here there be monsters* parts with thread-like tracks meandering their lonely way over featureless deserts or convoluted purple folds of mountains that squat on the surface like a frown or a warning - *"You're stuffed if you go here, mate!";* or selecting a remote part of the world using Google Maps, Satellite images, zooming in to skim across a desert surface noticing small tufts of thorn bush, salt-crusted pools of water with their spider web of animal *spoor*, occasional twin parallel tracks left by vehicles heading somewhere and nowhere, and no matter how long you trace them, following their random meanderings, they never reach anywhere other than, perhaps, another set of tracks heading who knows where. And you yearn with every fibre of your being just to *be* there, to follow them until they reach wherever they are going.

Although its conception was somewhat tentative, our next adventure bike trip was beginning to develop in the womb of our minds...

Just a thought:

If you'd like to skip the preparation and planning for this trip and just read about the journey itself, please feel free to skip ahead to the chapter "Touch-down in Kazakhstan - The adventure begins". Maybe come back to my philosophical musings afterwards, if you like.

You paid for it - do what you want; trust me, I won't mind.

Make Benefit Glorious Nation of Kazakhstan

When I opened the official Tajik consulate website to check visa details, up popped an advertisement for Viagra.

"Generic Cialis Viagra online without prescription ..." it said.

Must have been hacked.

No wonder Sasha Baron Cohen chose one of the 'Stans (Kazakhstan, actually) as the homeland of his fictional character Borat Sagdiyev for his spoof documentary: "Cultural Learnings of America for Make Benefit Glorious Nation of Kazakhstan".

Advertising Viagra on the official Tajik consulate website could have been a spoof written by Cohen himself but it was actually there!

Cohen's Borat reflects, in a way, the attitude of many Westerners towards the 'Stans and those who live there: somewhat backward and existing still in a forgotten limbo of an obscure part of the disintegrated USSR, a place where our conception of a Borat might live.

So, just like a country whose consulate advertises Viagra, Borat was born (according to Wikipedia and those nerdy souls who keep a record of these things) in the fictional village of Kuzcek in Kazakhstan. His parents were Asimbala Sagdiyev and Boltok the Rapist (who is also Borat's paternal grandfather, uncle and father-in-law). He claims his mother gave birth to him when she was nine years old. He has a thirteen-year-old son named Hooeylewis, twelve-year-old twin boys named Biram and Bilak, and seventeen grandchildren. His sister, Natalya, he assures us (with a certain degree of pride) is the "best prostitute in all of Kazakhstan"; Bilo, his disabled younger brother, is kept in a cage.

It isn't known how many times Borat has been married but one of his wives, Ludmilla, is said to have been shot by a hunter when he mistook her for a bear as she plowed the fields, and his former wife, Oksana, is reported to have been attacked and violated by a bear while taking his brother Bilo for a walk in the forest.

According to Cohen, Borat attended Astana University, where he studied English, Journalism, and Plague Research. During his studies, he claims to have created five new plagues which "killed over 5 million goats in Uzbekistan". Prior to this abortive dabbling in eugenics, Borat worked as an ice maker, gypsy catcher and computer maintenance engineer (specifically, removing dead birds which had nested in the vents in the computer's casing). He now works as a professional journalist and announcer on Kazakh television. In his spare time, he enjoys, amongst other things, disco dancing, spitting, shooting dogs and hunting Jews in his homeland.

So much for Borat.

Kazakhs are, understandably, not particularly happy about the film and its portrayal of their national culture. But having someone hack into your country's official website to advertise Viagra doesn't do much to convince us that people living in the 'Stans don't live lives that exhibit a faint resemblance to Borat's.

However, I have no doubt that, after we have traveled there and met the Kazakhs and Tajiks and Uzbeks and Kyrgyzs at first hand, the real Borats and their wives and children, they will become to us as special as the rural Russian people have become, with their generosity and earthy genuineness. It's all too easy to poke fun at people from a distance.

(But I seriously think someone ought to have a look at their website security or it will reinforce the stereotype that all Kazakhs are Borat clones.)

Harley-lovin' redneck

What is it about planning or embarking on a motorbike adventure that sets the pulse racing? Or riding a bike along a rough, deserted track, far from civilization?

Is it, as Trappist monk Thomas Merton says: *"One has to leave the world to discover it"*? - the world of your comfortable certainties, the daily routine that dulls the mind and spirit.

As I type this, I am drawn to Eliot's "Preludes" and his

> *"... eyes*
> *Assured of certain certainties,*
> *The conscience of a blackened street*
> *Impatient to assume the world."*

Too many people, despite being "impatient to assume the world" still live mundane lives that revolve like Eliot's ancient women who gather fuel in vacant lots.

I once read something in Bike & Track Magazine back in 1981 about a guy's passion for Harleys (and contempt for anything made by the Japanese). I loved the style of his writing, his bias so all-encompassing and assured, so I cut it out and have kept it tucked away in a sort of "Bits and Pieces that Tickle my Fancy" file ever since, revisiting it every few years for a chuckle. Even now I can picture the redneck with beer-froth on his unkempt beard, greasy leather waistcoat with chains and "Sons of Satan" in bold letters across the back, punching someone in the face because he dared to diss a Harley.

I don't know the guy's name but I'm sure he won't mind me using it.

Here is part of what he wrote:

"Upon approaching the machine your heart begins to beat a little faster and your palms get sweaty, your right leg trembles with anticipation. You rise up and come down precisely on the kick starter and the big twin rumbles into life; your heart beats still faster then settles down to a slow idle, like the bike. Ka WHOMP! Ka WHOMP! the motor says as it hits a tremendous lick on each stroke. You pull in the clutch, punch it in gear and you hear the warming familiar KA-CHUNK as the gears begin to mesh in place. You blip the throttle, throw the clutch out the window and you're on your way. It feels wonderful, s-o-o-o goooood, as they say in the skin books. Your eyes roll back in your head and your tongue rolls out the side of your mouth. Damn! this is nice, you think to yourself."

I understand what he's saying about the grunt look and sound of a Harley, something that hits you deep inside, enigmatic and mystical: it's not your heart - that's too shallow and simplistic; it's not your soul, although that's part of it too.

Your being?

The other evening I was riding home in the dark and cold from Huddersfield in the UK; the motorway, ascending steadily into the moors, was nose-to-tail cars. Then it started to snow. Soon the road was white, my visor was clogging up and I had to wipe the snow off every few seconds just so I could see the cars a few metres in front of me.

Then the bike began to slide; that ominous sensation transmitted up your legs, through your spine and into your head that whispers urgently to your autonomous nervous system, "Listen, my good buddy, just to let you know that your back wheel has decided to go a little sideways - not too bad at the moment - Whoah! That's the front wheel!" and I thought to myself: I really don't think it's a good idea to drop the bike on a snow-covered motorway during rush-hour traffic in poor visibility. What have I got myself into here?

But, underneath the fear was that frisson of excitement, the enjoyment of the danger, the heightened sensitivity to *life*, living in the moment. The feeling that, in some small way, you're the master of your own destiny (unless, of course, some idiot using a mobile phone takes you out with a truck).

And so often that feeling comes when you ride a bike. And the more extreme, the more remote the places you travel to, the greater the feeling. It's like a drug.

So, to get back to my one-eyed friend above, while I do feel that shortness of breath and faster pulse-rate when I hear a rugged Hogley-Dinkleson's *Ka-WOMP! Ka-WOMP!*, it's a loaded, long-distance-travelling, on/off-road big twin that gives me that thousand-yard stare and makes my fingers itch and a warm hollowness begin to form in my belly.

But I wouldn't do it on a Stroker. Despite my Hog-lovin' redneck's passion for Harleys *("If it ain't a Hog, it's spit, and that's it.")*, they are really for the open road, preferably tar. He can refer to Jap bikes disparagingly as "rice burners" and "Nip pieces of junk" but I love the reliability of Japanese engineering.

A Harley, according to my biased friend, might be *"more reliable than your mother and can be held together in her old age with baling wire and stove bolts, and that's something you can't do with your mother"* but I'd prefer a bike that doesn't need to be held together with baling wire at all; and the nimble fingers and inscrutable minds of our Oriental friends make amazingly reliable bikes.

And when stuck deep in snow or sand or teetering on the edge of a rocky slope, I give thanks to the Almighty for the Magic Button that fires up my engine without my having to kick it back to life, regardless of how macho the act of kick-starting an engine might be. To quote my eloquent friend just one more time: *"A stroker is SO BAD that when starting a Hog and you don't know what you're doing, it'll kick back, break your leg, rip you off its back and stomp you flatter 'n a squashed toad frog all in one deft motion. Don't let anybody tell you different, a stroker is BAAADD."*

I'd rather press a little black button, thank you very much, sir! (No disrespect intended. Please don't punch me.) Any one who has ridden off-road or along muddy green lanes until you are so exhausted that just lifting your mud-sodden boot onto the kick-start lever is an effort will know the blessing of the little magic button placed conveniently next to your right thumb.

I remember, a long time ago now, riding that notorious stretch of track in northern Kenya between Isiolo and Marsibit (where you are supposed to ride in convoy with a bunch of trucks interspersed with army vehicles bristling with armed soldiers against the bands of Shifta who lurk in the area and prey on travellers - but Gareth and I soon left the convoy and rode our bikes all day alone) when I was so exhausted that kick-starting my aged XT500 was almost beyond my limited reserves of strength. As evening approached, after my umpteenth fall on that horrible, rutted excuse for a road, I could only manage at best two kicks before I had barely the strength to hold the bike up, let alone start it. Fortunately my seventeen-year-old son was with me and, I blush to admit it, on a few occasions I allowed him to kick that big old single-cylinder, 500cc engine to life for me. Then, I would have given my pension for the old Magic Button.

I call it a "horrible, rutted excuse for a road", but I'd ride it again tomorrow. In all its roughness and the scars that both Gareth and I still carry on our legs from two bad falls that day, it's a road that sticks in the memory, that is fixed there forever by its ruggedness, by the sheer adventure of riding it - unlike a million miles of bland tar road that blend formlessly into the subconscious and is forgotten.

Lose the Girlfriend

So, perhaps this long digression will give some insight into why just mouthing the names: Kyrgyzstan... Uzbekistan... Tajikistan... Kazakhstan... Turkmenistan... as we began to plan our next trip filled me with a disturbing wanderlust for remote desert places, rocky tracks that wind their precarious way up the sides of mountains, vistas that fade into that smudged purple of distance; of smoky rooms and faces etched deeply with the strain of living secluded and difficult lives. I want to feel the tyres shift and slide a little beneath me, feel the wind and the rain in my face, coax my bike across a landscape that is not desensitised, homogenised by a layer of tar.

Because that's the adventure of it.

That's what makes living more alive.

And it's only when you've been shivering your ass off on a long, rain-slicked road that you *truly* enjoy the companionable warmth of a fire; only when you've experienced the lonely isolation of the road that you fully appreciate the welcome of a stranger's open door.

As Brett Houle wrote "Iron and Air", a magazine that celebrates everything about the creative spirit entwined in motorcycling:

"Complete and stupid happiness isn't the only way. Life will always deliver a mixed bag. But in it is the richness... Sometimes you need some pain to get to the joy.

"And so love your fate. Lose the girlfriend. Lose your mind. Don't eat for three days. Freeze. Go to jail. Get married. Wake for sunrise. Endure. For if you're going to do it, there is no other way and there is no other feeling. As Bukowski said, 'You will be alone with the gods, and the nights will flame with fire. You will ride life straight to perfect laughter.'

"Here's to riding more than we wrench. Here's to over the hills and far away. Here's to staying fully alive."

You can't express it better than that.

And so, the trip continues to develop, from zygote to embryo:

10 February - Ordered maps of the 'Stans and Ukraine and 2nd hand copy of Lonely Planet: Central Asia.

15 February - The maps have arrived and I am a third of the way through Lonely Planet. A rough plan has formed: Fly the bikes to Almaty in Kazakhstan, allow three weeks to explore the 'Stans and then head home via Ukraine and Russia. Five weeks in total.

Sorted.

Just an approximate jab of a finger on a map spread out on the table, Gareth and I absorbed in its convoluted folds and indistinct lines: here... then here... then there... and see what happens once we get there. Allow serendipity and the randomness of chance encounters to mould the trip as we go along. That's the best way to travel.

So long as nothing goes wrong.

Like Russia usurping Crimea, perhaps? *(Or a rock slide...)*

A few days later and all hell is breaking loose in Ukraine with scores of protestors shot dead by police in Kiev's Independence Square. If you're a tyrant and instruct the police to start shooting protestors, you'd better make sure you win... because if the protestors absorb the killing and keep coming back, then *they* win and they'll hunt you down and hang you.

The protestors came back.

Viktor Yanukovych ran.

The Russians are not happy.

How much guts must it take to keep coming back, facing the bullets, crouched behind small pieces of tin and burning tyre barricades, dead and wounded lying around you in the street?

If this continues, we might have to go the long northern route round on our return journey, missing Ukraine altogether.

The "fear" factor

J.Mummolo wrote somewhere:

"A journey is not a singular event, but a relentless chain of discoveries. With each crook in the path, each passing shadow into blazing sun, we are called upon to be present. To stay in one place is to leave whole tracts of oneself undiscovered."

As he suggests, adventure travel lends itself to self discovery. This has some resonance with my past experiences planning and embarking on motorcycle trips as well as this one. As I research the 'Stans through which we will be travelling, I am already embarking on my own "chain of discoveries", something that will continue with each icy dawn somewhere high up in the Tian Shan mountains or in the flesh-melting heat of the Kyzylkum Desert - I have no idea; our route hasn't been planned yet.

Implicit in the term 'adventure' is *fear*, something that keeps the blood racing. And we all seek adventure of some kind to make life more interesting, more stimulating (well, most of us - my wife doesn't; she *genuinely* doesn't understand). Little children scream their fear on fairground rides called *Doom, Mega-Death, Euthanasia* or something similarly encouraging, and then plead with their parents - hearts beating, eyes wildly dilated - that they be allowed to go again.

It's the fear that makes it special, holds the experience in one's memory.

Like a drug, we always need more: travel the world in search of a bigger wave to surf, a higher waterfall to kayak down; lean just a little further into a corner until you feel the tyres momentarily lose their grip and a knee touch the tar; sit closer to the silverback gorilla, knowing that at any moment this wild creature could smash every bone in your body in a fit of irritable pique. It's as if, incongruously, the closer we are to death the more alive we feel. You never get that feeling sitting in front of the telly watching re-runs of the Jerry Springer Show.

For me, the thought of planning a long motorcycle journey without some degree of fear would be boring. It would remove that *frisson* of the unknown, the unexpected, the threat that heightens the senses and makes an adventure of life. I'm not talking about the kind of fear that some travellers face, the get-it-wrong-and-you-die kind of fear. I admire people who attempt trips like that but I don't really want to be one of them. But a certain degree of threat - whether this comes from the people who inhabit the lands or the terrain through which you will travel - makes the pulse race a little and, when you do come through with interesting tales to tell, you feel just that much more in touch with life.

With this in mind, I know my father was very worried when we decided to push on, my brother and I just 12 and 14 years old, through the remote Gorongosa region between the Save and Buzi Rivers in Mocambique on our 1200-mile bicycle ride from Durban to Beira in 1966, knowing that we had 100 miles of soft sand to struggle through, pushing our laden bicycles along indistinct tracks with lions prowling about in the bush and tsetse flies biting the hell out of us. But we made it through in three very uncomfortable, memorable days and, in the process, discovered things about ourselves that would have lain hidden had we not attempted the adventure.

There was a great deal of fear when I decided to take my 17-year-old son on our first bike trip together, across Africa on two rather worn XT500s in 1997. I remember, while still debating with myself whether to risk the trip, phoning a man who had done the trans-Africa thing, expressing my concerns and my fear of exposing my son to the dangers that one expects when crossing Africa, and he said to me, long before Nike: *"Just do it. You'll never forget it."*

We did and we haven't. And, I'm proud to say, eighteen years later we're still doing it.

And I must admit to being fearful when I planned my first trip into Russia; and even after three Russian journeys, my heart still beats a little faster when I approach a Russian border post. But it's that sense of the unknown and the unexpected that makes Russia special and draws me back again and again.

Both Gareth and I were more than apprehensive when the track we had been following across the desert in Southern Morocco disappeared and we didn't know what to do: give up and head back to the safety of the known, to the certainty of fuel and people and houses - or press on, hoping the single GPS waypoint somewhere in the vast emptiness of the desert that Gareth had downloaded from the Internet before we left would not turn out to be a chimera and leave us stranded far from a road or a village when our fuel ran out. But looking back now, that fear made the journey more memorable, more exciting.

So I read the warnings about extreme heat in the Karakum and Kyzylkum deserts that will kill you if your vehicle breaks down; the advice to keep clear of policemen in the 'Stans because of their tendency to arbitrarily arrest you in order to extort a bribe; false accusations of drink driving; of jumpy, Kalashnikov-carrying soldiers close to the Afgan and Chinese borders; land mines laid between the Uzbek-Tajik and Uzbek-Kyrgyz borders and my heart rate increases just a little and my yearning to go there increases.

So - the 'Stans and back to the UK through Russia, Ukraine and Poland...

Four and a half months to go.

25 February - Finished my first run through of Lonely Planet: Central Asia. Lots of highlighting. Made a long list of "Must Do's" which Gareth and I will discuss at some time when we start looking at possible routes. My 2nd hand copy of LP was published seven years ago so much of the information might be out of date. We shall see.

It has become quite clear that Turkmenistan and Uzbekistan are going to be non-starters on this trip. Turkmenistan mainly because one is required to hire a "guide" who accompanies you everywhere for the whole time you are in the country. Not going to happen. And Uzbekistan will have to be cut out because the main attraction on this trip would have been crossing the Kyzylkum desert. Advice on this is fairly straightforward: *Do not attempt to cross the Kyzylkum desert in the furnace of mid-summer. Day-time temperatures in excess of 40 degrees last from mid-July to the end of August.*

We've only got five weeks and it will take two weeks just to ride home from Almaty. Gareth had a quick look on Google Maps and plotted a shortest distance return home through Kazakhstan, Russia, Ukraine, Poland, etc and it is over 6000km. We'll wear out a set of tyres before we get home and, judging from past trips, I'll wear out a set of rear brake pads too. We are considering putting knobblies on for the mountains and then replacing them with on/off road tyres for the trip back.

10 March - Posted off passports and forms for our Russian visas. Just hope they reach the Russian embassy before they shut the doors and shout *"Nyet!"* to Brits applying for visas with the Crimea debacle in progress.

Further preparations and some thoughts about Crimea

No Russian visa yet. This evening I was listening to the BBC and heard the following: *"Russian soldiers are massing on the Ukraine border just two to three days' march from the Ukrainian capital, Kiev. German Chancellor Angela Merkel met today with Bronislaw Komorowski, president of Poland, discussing what sanctions to apply against Russia. Visa and travel bans for senior officials are being discussed. Komorowski expressed his concern about Polish sovereignty and Nato is responding. Today F16 fighter planes from America landed in Poland in a gesture of support."*

Where is this heading?

Later Oleksandr Turchynov, Ukrainian interim president, said, *"How can you negotiate when you've got the barrel of a gun pointing at your head - especially if the gun is held by a Russian?"*

He's got a point.

Looked at the visa requirements for Georgia on the Net. Not needed for UK citizens. If Ukraine falls apart, we might have to come home via Russia, Georgia and Turkey.

C'est la vie.

But after the end of the Cold War and the collapse of the whole Communist experiment, one can understand something of Putin's motivations. Russia, for so long equal in power with the US, tethered to each other on the leash of Mutually Assured Destruction, within a decade has found herself toothless and poor with a seemingly unstoppable China on her doorstep. And after the embarrassment of Yeltsin and his drunken escapades, one can see the attraction of Putin the hard man - with his bare-back, bare-chested horse riding and his judo, his hunting in the wilderness, piloting a hang glider and riding a Harley - for so many Russians yearning to recapture their past glory; understandable why he sent in troops to occupy Georgia and now Crimea, determined not to lose even more influence and territory to an ever expanding West.

And, in a way, although one cannot agree with it, one cannot but admire the Russians' sometimes suicidal determination to protect and defend their beloved Motherland, a whatever-it-takes mindset that values the preservation of the State above the lives and liberty of its citizens. Jailing Pussy Riot's Nadezhda Tolokonnikova and Maria Alyokhina for publicly criticizing Putin, and charging Greenpeace activists with "piracy" for their protest against Russian oil drilling in the Pechora Sea makes that clear.

Don't challenge us or you'll get hurt! Putin said between the lines to the whole world just last week. *And all of you in the West can simper and tutt-tutt and threaten as much as you like because it don't mean nothin', bud. We do it our way. And don't threaten us because, if you try to punish us for Crimea, we'll get hurt but you'll get hurt too.*

And we can take it.

Stalingrad should tell you that...

Interestingly, while most of the Russian bikers we met in our previous trip to Archangel and Murmansk mourned the loss of

Russia's past greatness, they all seemed to dislike with a passion the autocratic Putin and the way he has put himself above the man in the street.

They did feel that Stalin had been misjudged by history, though - particularly Western history. And they are not alone.

But back to Putin: A brief extract from Sasha's (the Russian biker who befriended us on our 2012 Russian trip and with whom we keep in contact) email to me last week as we tentatively explored the possibility of meeting up in the 'Stans and travelling together makes his dislike clear in his delightful self-taught English:

"All the more so that political rat race round Ukraine can make visa obtainment more complicated for Russians due to mr. Putin and his team. Needless to say about quotation of Rubble last weeks. :(I'm thinking about Altai mountains... what you think? Soon!"

And maybe that's why when travelling through Russia you always have a slight feeling of fear (well, at least, *I* do), of looking over your shoulder to check whether someone in a uniform is watching and making notes.

Russian visas arrived today. For a while there I felt as if we were running at a rapidly closing door. With Dmitry Medvedev stating yesterday that "...there will be blood" where Crimea is concerned and the EU imposing travel bans on some twenty Russian and Ukranian officials, I was expecting the Russians to play tit-for-tat and stop issuing visas. Fortunately for us they didn't. Of course, when we arrive at the Russian border in a few months' time, whether they'll honour our crisp new visas and let us in - that's another story.

Bought one-way tickets to Almaty in Kazakhstan and posted visa applications to Tajikistan and Kyrgyzstan embassies.

Stumbled upon an article in The Times headed "Dictator sent men to beat up his daughter".

Turns out it was about Uzbekistan.

Evidently Gulnara Karimova, daughter of Uzbekistan's "repressive dictator" Islam Karimov, abruptly disappeared from public view five weeks ago. It seems she is being kept under house arrest on her father's orders, along with her fifteen-year-old daughter and that she had been beaten up. In a smuggled letter that reached the BBC, she says: "How *naïve* I was to think that the rule of law exists in this country. The reason for this Pinochet-style persecution is that I dared to speak up about things that millions are quiet about."

Having accused her father and his sidekicks of corruption, he - she claims - sent twenty to thirty men to her apartment where she and her partner were beaten up.

The Times Moscow correspondent, Helen Womack, states: "Mr Karimov's government has one of the world's worst human rights records, along with endemic corruption and persecution of minorities. In the most notorious case, in 2002, two prisoners were boiled alive."

Maybe Sasha Baron Cohen was closer to the truth than he realised.

Better not do anything to upset the Uzbeks, then.

******

Quotes from ordinary Russians' yearning for the stability provided by Stalin, taken from David Satter's book: "It was a Long Time Ago and it Never Happened Anyway":

Konstantin Kalachev, deputy mayor of Volgograd: "There is an absence of moral leaders. People hate the hypocrisy they see every day. People go to work honestly and see that for this they get nothing. Stalin lived modestly. He did not accumulate property. He did not use his authority to enrich himself. He was bloodthirsty but honest. He murdered honestly..."

Dmitri Krayukhin, Russian human rights activist, 2012: "People see that it is hard to find work, that the authorities can do what they want. They see corruption and banditry, and they don't see any other way to deal with it but repression... They say that under Stalin, corrupt people were shot."

"Stalin freed the whole world... the Americans destroyed the Indians. But they don't cry and cover themselves with ashes. Why should we?"

Yelena Silantieva, editor of the local weekly newspaper Den za Dyem: "Stalin wanted to be equal among equals. He sacrificed his own son. Today, not a single oligarch has a son in the army. He had no palaces. He did not take more than he was entitled to. When people see how officials take bribes and build palaces, they say if only Stalin were alive, this wouldn't be happening."

Lyudmilla Zelenikina, history teacher: "In Soviet times, people were kinder, souls were more open. There was pride in the country. The world took note of our opinion, and people felt that they were part of this great country. Now, people feel more pain. Mutual help, which was always typical of Russians, disappears, even in the countryside."

The World's Great Adventure Motorcycle Routes

Gareth lent me a glossy, coffee-table book someone gave him for Christmas: *The World's Great Adventure Motorcycle Routes*. In it were some articles on the 'Stans.

It's good to know that where we are planning to go in a few months' time is regarded by those in the know as one of the World's Greats - although in the same book they've included an article on *The Garden Route* just north of Cape Town. Now the name itself would seem to suggest that this isn't a heart-stopping part of the world to go adventure motorcycling in.

"Where're you headed, mate?"

"The Garden Route - you know, near Cape Town."

"Wooah! The *Garden Route!* - sounds tough, man! You take care now!"

The Garden Route is where retired couples wearing cardigans and sensible shoes drive their Fiestas for afternoon tea.

OK, I exaggerate a little. But I don't really regard a little spin just north of the most sophisticated city in the whole of Africa an "Adventure Motorcycle Route" so maybe they've got the 'Stans wrong too.

Anyway, a few snippets from the "London to Beijing" article by Kevin and Julia Sanders included in the book. Part of their trip was through the 'Stans:

"...add to this river crossings, landslides, minefields, heavy snow and with Afghanistan sometimes a mere twenty metres to your right, this road is what adventure bike riding is all about... Given what is to come, you don't want to leave Dushanbe without ensuring the bikes have some major attention, including new knobbly tyres, and that you get extra supplies... There is no easy route to Kalaikhum - either way will turn into a goat track or a muddy quagmire, with the road climbing to altitude and clinging to the side of a cliff face, and you'll not avoid a river crossing either... Landslides are almost as common as river crossings. On our second day on the Pamir, two separate slides had blocked the road. One was impassable until an ancient grader had done five hours' worth of pushing and scraping. Then, within hours, a massive truck blocked the route, grounded on another landslide it couldn't get over. You can see very quickly how hard it is to predict travel in the Pamir Mountains... The Silk Road is the essence of motorcycle adventure travel. It takes you out of your comfort zone completely - to regions where English is not spoken... where the writing is completely unintelligible, where you cannot afford to be ill or injured, where freedom of movement is restricted and political stability can be a smokescreen, where credit cards don't work and you can't flick open your mobile and expect it to work... Getting fuel is never certain and being able to sort your bike out for yourself if it goes wrong is essential. It's an unpredictable road journey - extremes abound, whether it's the late winters and snowbound passes or natural disasters such as landslides and earthquakes. This is motorcycle adventure travel at its best. What more could you ask for?"

Yes, I think we can give this one a try.

The second article from the book is *Adventure Riding in the 'Stans* by Krzysztof Samborski, who writes like someone who travels this kind of terrain regularly, giving information with an off-hand nonchalance.

Krzysztof writes: *"An adventure into Central Asia is not to be underestimated, with the sheer scale of the area being its first consideration: Kazakhstan is the ninth largest country in the world and is some eleven times bigger than the UK; the combined size of the 'Stans is equivalent to more than twice the area of Mexico. Second, the nature of the terrain, particularly the mountains, is very different from what most adventure riders are accustomed to; while what many people would define as a 'road', a 'border crossing' or a 'procedure' are quite different from other adventure destinations."*

(I wonder what he means by a "procedure"? I hope it's not something policemen wearing dark glasses do to you while wearing rubber gloves.)

Krzysztof continues: *"The Pamir Mountains represent the meeting point of three great mountain ranges: the Tian Shan, the Karakorum/Himalays and the Hindu Kush. The Pamir Highway is known as the second highest altitude international highway in the world, and it has been used for hundreds of years as one of the only viable routes through the Pamir Mountains, forming a vital link on the ancient Silk Road trade route. The route has been off-limits to travellers until recently... paved in places, but heavily damaged by erosion, earthquakes, landslides and avalanches..."* (On the Bartang Valley) *"Research this route carefully before attempting it - it's vulnerable to landslides which can keep the road blocked for weeks. The likelihood of meeting other vehicles is minimal. Solo journeys are discouraged, given the remoteness, and it's imperative to take all provisions as well as additional fuel."*

My heart rate has increased slightly as I type this. I can feel the bike under me and my mind is filled with the silent presence of remote, snow-topped mountains...

Tajik and Kazakh visas have arrived as well as the GBAO permit to travel through the sensitive border regions close to China, Pakistan and Afghanistan. But it's only a stamp in the passport and, as far as I have been able to find out, there is supposed to be a specified list noted down: *"...make sure you get all the regions you want to visit (these are Ishkashim, Murgab, Vani, Darvaz, Shugnan, Rushan and Roshtqala)."* I can just picture a uniformed man casually holding a *Kalashnikov* in his calloused hands, pupils opium-dilated, stabbing a finger at my passport and screaming unintelligibly into our faces that we've strayed into a highly sensitive border area without the correct paperwork and we are going to be incarcerated in some rat-infested hole until we can pay him five hundred gazillion somoni (which, I understand from Wikipedia, is the national currency of Tajikistan).

Will have to make some enquiries.

On the strength of the issued visas, I took out my maps, Lonely Planet Central Asia and *The World's Great Adventure Motorcycle Routes* and marked up the maps with some potential routes, making little notes and annotations as *aides-memoire* for when we're there.

To be honest, I have little idea of what to expect but, as always, local conditions on the ground will dictate just where we go and how far off the beaten track we will push. The marked routes are just a starting point. I know there will be river crossings - which should be interesting: *"...during early summer (June and July) melt water can make river crossings dangerous in the mountain areas."* (Well, we planned *that* well, heading into the mountains in June and July.)

We will definitely start off with knobblies fitted and keep our on-off road tyres for the long slog back through Kazakhstan, Russia and Ukraine.

The Bartang Valley: *"...stark and elemental... at times the fragile road is only perilously inches between the raging river below and sheer cliffs above."*

Yes, note that one down...

"Past Savnob, a road of sorts continues on to Kokj Jar and Murgab but the road is in a very bad condition and only worth contemplating at the end of summer and with a reliable 4WD." (Should be a doddle on a bike, then.) *"As one local told us: 'The road to Koki Jar is fine but at the end of the trip both the car and the driver will be destroyed'."*

It's the height that concerns me a little - how will the bikes perform over the At-Baital Pass at 15,300 ft? Should I think of re-jetting the carb? Altitude sickness (hypobaropathy or "the altitude bends"), is a greater concern because it kills. *("For the most part, the Pamirs are too high for human habitation.")* If you get it - Altitude Sickness, that is - there isn't really any solution other than getting to lower ground as quickly as possible - and when you've collapsed somewhere deep in the Pamir Mountains with your brain swelling up and coming out your nose, there's not much that can be done about it, especially as the Pamirs, supposedly, are *"the least explored mountain range on earth".*

I spent an anxious half hour before I got to sleep last night wondering whether I'd have the strength to lift my unconscious son onto my bike and ride with him to a safe altitude; whether I would be able to hold him on the bike or have to strap him to myself with our emergency tow rope - and then realising that trying to cross a river strapped together would be somewhat akin to jumping off a high building without a parachute. Even though Gareth is a man now, I still feel as responsible for him as I felt for the seventeen-year-old I took trans-Africa with me so many years ago, remembering my fear in case something went wrong and he died on the trip.

Maybe I'm worrying too much here; we'll just do it.

While I was reading up on these possible routes (and boning up on Altitude Sickness on the Internet), Gareth arrived on his

KTM for a visit. He checked the potential routes I had marked on my map and agreed that I'd pretty much identified the ones he had earmarked from his reading. He felt, though, that perhaps the Pamir Highway was by now somewhat *passé* (he didn't use that word, but it was what he meant) - the route that most riders who attempt the 'Stans take as a matter of course. He is looking for something more remote, more unusual, more off the beaten track, and I'm happy about that. For Gareth - and I suppose for me too - the conventional is just a tad boring. But who knows - the Pamir Highway itself might well be all we anticipated and test us to our limits.

We'll find out when we get there.

But what would disappoint me greatly would be to discover that suddenly the 'Stans and, in particular, the Pamir Highway, has become *the* destination of choice for bikers, *de rigueur* for those of us looking for adventure; then how long before quaint Tajik "Biker Friendly" cafes start springing up in the mountains and *kallapush*-wearing Tajik men with plastic smiles flag you down at the entrance to villages calling, "Welcome, my friend, how are you? Good! Good! You want food? Hotel? I have a friend can take you on hike, sleep in yurt, traditional dancing after food just small extra cost, no problem, you like?"

Then I must look somewhere else to travel where our sometimes questionable Western lifestyle has not yet started to unravel the unique social fabric to be found amongst people living in far-off, inaccessible places.

(I know you are thinking: *But* you, *my friend, are the beginning of that rot...*)

I realise that - and I don't have an answer other than to travel lightly, treat all who live there with respect, try not to flaunt our seeming wealth, blend in wherever possible, absorb as much of their culture as I can during our fleeting visit and try to leave behind a positive impression of ours.

How *pious* does that sound? Sorry about that. All I can say in mitigation is, well... it's true.

Anyway, Gareth pointed to the map lying open on my bed and traced his finger along an interesting looking track just north of the Wakhan Corridor, a narrow panhandle of Afgan territory between Northern Pakistan and Tajikistan. The track starts off as a continuous, narrow red line on the map but then, somewhere high up in the mountains, it stutters into a series of small dotted lines that seem to meander about for a while as if they are lost and trying to find a way out (but probably not as lost as we will be if we attempt it). This track begins at Murgab, the highest town in Tajikistan, following the Aksu River valley before it turns sharply east, deeper into the mountains; somewhere along the dotted line there is a pass marked at 4427m - the Yangidvan; the track then wanders a bit further until it reaches Lake Zorkol then follows the Afgan border until, eventually, it reaches the Pamir Highway again at Kharguah.

Mark that track, please.

Then there's a much smaller road that takes a short cut between the northern and southern loops of the Pamir Highway between Khorog and Sasyk-Kel, initially following the Shokh Dara Valley. Just at the start of the 4X4 track, evidently, in 2002 a massive landslide wiped out the village of Dasht, killing twenty four people and diverting the river. This route also degenerates into a dotted line on the map which is *"an old 4X4 track"* across the mountains to rejoin the main Pamir Highway, *"but there is a difficult river crossing for which you'll need a high-clearance 4X4... ask herders for the best route"*.

Mark that track too (I think).

Later that evening I found myself reflecting on those two remote tracks through the mountains and felt again that strangely compelling numbness and explosive *life* that comes over you just before you leap off a gorge with a bungee cord tied about your ankles or lift off a steep slope with a paraglider canopy tugging and fluttering in the wind above you, that feeling of heightened sensitivity that I was trying to capture at the beginning of this travelogue when referring to the joy most of us feel when we allow ourselves to face something new and slightly dangerous, something that takes us outside our comfort zone and sets the pulse racing.

The trip is taking on a more tangible shape now.

I can almost feel it.

Small creatures are beginning to shrug themselves out of their chrysalises and stretch their multicoloured, gossamer wings in the region of my abdomen...

Well, you know what I mean.

Ukraine - again

Listening to the radio this morning before I got up, I heard a report about orchestrated attacks by pro-Russian militants who have occupied key government buildings in a number of east Ukrainian towns. Ukraine's acting president has pledged a full-scale "anti-terrorist operation" involving the army. Russia warns that any use of force in east Ukraine could scupper crisis talks due this week; the West accuses Moscow of inciting the trouble and America threatens "additional consequences". The Kremlin denies the charge.

This East-West bickering might seriously interfere with a certain motorcycle trip in the near future...

Gentle Reader, I get the feeling that about this time in the narrative you seem to be asking: Where is this travelogue going? I've been reading for *ages* and the trip hasn't even begun yet.

I understand.

I'm asking that question myself - and I'm writing the thing.

Trust me, I didn't plan it this way. It just kind of *evolved* - like most of our journeys do. When the 'Stans trip was conceived, multiplying and mutating like a living thing, I felt compelled to start writing about it even though it was still six months away.

Many writers claim that they don't choose to write a book - the book chooses them. When I was writing novels, I found that, as I was nearing the end of one book, out of the many ideas sloshing about in my brain that might one day emerge as a book, one, like an insistent chick jostling in the nest with its hungry siblings, would stick its scrawny neck out, open its gaping beak and scream, "Me! Me!" until I had to give in and feed it.

This travelogue was similar, in a way. *Is* similar. It seems to *want* to be written - and who am I to say no?

So I started writing.

And after a short while I thought it might be interesting (and only you, Gentle Reader, can be the judge of that) to share with you the gestation of the trip, the initial conception (Gareth's email to me with the attached photo and *"Next year?"*); then follow this with how the journey coalesced, our plans, my thoughts and feelings, growing anticipation, the somewhat cursory research, preparing the bikes and shipping them and then, finally, the trip itself, born and delivered (to flog an already over-worked metaphor), with a life of its own.

And, believe me, these trips - like the book - have a tendency to head off on interesting tangents at a moment's notice - and, as I think I've said before, that's what makes them so exciting: The unpredictability of life on the road in strange, far-off places.

Of course, it might not work. Many of you might already have dumped this book in the bin with a yawn of disgust and are, at this very moment, vicariously riding along with some intrepid soul astride his BMW heading for a distant, snake-infested wilderness with a dark-eyed wench (whom he came across hitch-hiking along a dusty stretch of road) clinging to him on the pillion.

Well, my story is what it is. An ordinary man, somewhat long in the tooth, heading off on an adventure with his son. I think the action will come later. (Hopefully not *too* much action - just enough to keep it interesting.)

We shall see. I hope that you will feel, by the end, that you've got your few quid's worth.

Been working on a full service of the bike and, with Gareth, going through tools and spares for the trip. We've got all necessary spanners for both bikes plus two spare tubes each, puncture repair kit, electric pump and tyre irons, spare cables routed and zip-tied in place, clutch lever, steel putty, bulbs and a selection of nuts and bolts, cable ties, tow strap; new brake pads. My chain and sprockets are OK - only a few months old - and we've ordered new knobblies for both bikes.

Gareth is working on securing his two fuel containers and panniers to the KTM. Like me, he enjoys personalising the bike himself rather than just ordering hair-raisingly expensive pannier sets, some of which don't give you much change out of £1000. A second-hand set of soft panniers/dry bags can be sourced for about fifty bucks and then attached to the bike using a simple welded frame. In the event of a fall, the soft luggage absorbs the impact and distorts whereas the more expensive, rigid aluminium panniers will break. It's not being cheapskate; we just like tinkering around with our own designs, adapting them to carry our luggage securely and keeping the weight as low as is reasonably possible.

Read this psalm this morning before I got up to see what the day had to offer and it resonated as if there was a presence right next to me mouthing the words; into my mind came a picture of a remote dirt road wandering through precipitous rocky valleys and I thought (or spoke aloud, I can't remember, like Samuel), "You talking to me, God?"

You yourself have recorded my wanderings.
Put my tears in Your bottle.
Are they not in Your records?
Then my enemies will retreat on the day when I call.
This I know: God is for me ...
In God I trust: I will not fear.

What can man do to me?
For You delivered me from death,
even my feet from stumbling,
to walk before God in the light of life...

Got out my old Russian language course cassette tapes, dusted them off and loaded the first into my cassette player, lay back on my bed and began to listen to the old familiar phrases ... *"Dobryj dyen. Minya zavoot..."*

A few years ago I came to the conclusion that, although having been a language teacher all my life, learning a new language is simply beyond me. Or maybe I'm just not prepared to put in the hours, secure in the knowledge that pretty much anywhere in the world someone will have a smattering of English (and most children, in my experience, can parrot, "How are you? What is your name? Manchester United!", hoping for a *petit cadeau*). Even when no mutually shared language can be found, so much meaningful conversation can be held using gestures and a smile. I tried really hard to learn just the basics of Russian for my first solo trip and found that my stumbling attempts were always appreciated. But I have a very poor memory for names and this includes remembering new vocabulary so, after my second Russian trip I gave up, realising that I wasn't really learning a *language* at all, just memorising lists of words and phrases which I was seldom able to reconfigure into original sentences. Perhaps my greatest success, though, was, when attempting to buy insurance in Murmansk, I was quoted a stupidly high price and managed to tell them, in Russian, that it was too expensive. They looked at the figures, had a short conflab and wrote on a piece of paper a figure that was about a tenth of their first offer. That made me feel great.

But I also felt like an idiot when, after a chance meeting with a group of very drunk soldiers who were interested in my bike and where I came from, I rode away calling out a cheery, *"Zdrastvuytye!"* instead of *Dasvidaniya*, forgetting all I had learned in the heat of the moment and mixing my words. Basically I had called out a cheery, *"Hello!"* as I rode away and, until I realised my mistake, I wondered why the soldiers were giving me a somewhat sideways look.

But it's good to be able to show people through whose country you are travelling that you have made some effort to learn their language and etiquette so that, at the very least, you can confer the dignity of a greeting or a goodbye, a smattering of basic communication, and not ride roughshod over their sensibilities, perhaps unintentionally dishonouring their religious beliefs or insulting them through ignorance of their customs. I believe all travellers ought to show at least that degree of respect.

So, I lie on my bed and mutter the Russian phrases into the emptiness of my room, having imaginary conversations that I hope to remember in a few months' time when asking directions somewhere high in the mountains where a rough, wind-swept track diverges and fuel is running low...

ICON Motorsport and Sponsorship

Got home from a three-week visit to my family in South Africa to find a large box just arrived from America. Christmas has come early!

I opened the box like a little kid at a party. Our sponsored kit had arrived.

Let it be said that I'm not usually interested in mucking about with sponsorship. I can cover the cost of my trips so long as we live and travel frugally so why bother? But Gareth and his business partner have developed a first-name relationship with the owner of the massive Icon Motorsports company in the USA through their marketing of a cleaner/de-greaser they have branded "EAT MY DIRT" (great product - you should buy some!). Icon Motorsport are motorcycle helmet and clothing manufacturers who have just launched a range of gear, Raiden, moving from the street into the adventure touring market. Gareth wondered whether they might be interested in featuring two ordinary guys travelling through remote regions wearing their gear so he put together a proposal showing photographs of our Russian and Morocco trips and sent it to Icon.

Within a week they had emailed their agreement, telling us to look at their product range on the Internet and select what we wanted.

Whooo! Thanks - we'll have one of those... and one of those... and one of those, please! They didn't specify just what kit they were prepared to sponsor so we chanced our arm and selected it all: boots, trousers, jacket, gloves and helmet. A week later came the email: "We'll just go with the helmets and jackets this time and see how it goes"!

Understandable. I mean, who are we and, really, why should they give us anything? The helmets have a Star Wars look about them; the jackets classy. Gareth and I decided we'd just have to put up with looking and riding like posers for a while with our flash new kit.

I like Icon's style. I like Ernie and New Guy as they ride their custom-built bikes like total idiots around the desert and through deserted factories, killing zombies and terrorists, nutters you admire because they've got the balls to ride the bikes on the edge in a way you never could.

I'm not flattering these guys because they sponsored us. I genuinely like what I see - people who manufacture riding gear but who look like mechanics with dirt under their nails, who seem to come to work to have a jolly, like, "Hey, laugh off designing clothes today - let's customise us a bike and then call Ernie and New Guy and make a film!"

And so, from their headquarters in Portland, Oregon, which looks more like a garage than a clothing manufacturer/warehouse, have come their custom-built bikes: The Dromedarii (Triumph Tiger 800XC); The Iron Lung ("... the most beautiful and ugly thing we've ever built"); the Low Down and Shifty (1974 Yamaha XS650); the Magnificent Bastard (1998 Honda CF1000R); the Quartermaster (2012 Ural Solo ST); Thunder Chunky (1994 Kawasaki ZX-7); the Operator (1999 Ducati 900SS) and The Roach (1986 Harley Sportster) amongst others.

And then they go play on them. It seems like it's bikes first, gear second - which is as it should be, come to think about it.

From their website: *"Our crashes are vicious street episodes. We aren't talking about some lame gravel trap slide on the inside of turn three. No grassy run-offs, no air fences, no corner workers. Ours are more like two lanes of oncoming and a bus-like encounter that makes you re-think this whole motorcycling thing... But for all our effort there will come a time when it's just you and the tarmac. A solitary statistical tumble... As a tribute to the select group of Icon abrasion and impact experts, we offer a token of our appreciation - Busted and Broken. Earned the hard way. Not available in a store near you. If you've gone down in Icon gear, then send us your story and pictures..."*

I hope on this trip we don't experience too many "statistical tumbles" or become "abrasion and impact experts" with photographs to post on the Icon website.

First sponsored kit ever.

No, I lie. I got some sponsorship once before, when I was teaching at Ixopo High School in Natal, South Africa, a small country village in the Midlands. Many of the lads I taught came from local farming stock and had grown up riding off-road bikes around their parents' farms. I had taken pupils up Sani Pass in my 4X4 into Lesotho on a few occasions to hike up Thaba Ntlenyana which, at 3482m, is Southern Africa's highest peak south of Mt Kilimanjaro.

On one of our hikes I wondered whether I could get a bike to the top of Thaba Ntlenyana. That was in 1987.

I recruited some of my pupils - Neil Camp (15), and John Jung, Ross Ollerman and Quinton van Jaarsveld (all 14) - and, nine months later, we made the first trip. Despite one of the boys falling ill and another's bike breaking a chain and smashing a hole in the aluminium sump on a rock (which we patched with duct tape) we finally made it to the top, just the final, eight foot high promontory to scale, too steep and rocky to make it up without help. Neil Camp was the first to attempt it. With the rest of us balanced precariously on either side of a narrow, rocky gully which led up to the peak in case something went wrong,

Neil hit the ridge, almost flipping upside down, but we dragged his bike up the last few feet; then we man-handled my KDX onto the peak as well. Positioning the two bikes together, we unfurled the Ixopo High School banner which we had brought with us and held it proudly against the buffeting wind for a group photograph. Nine months of planning had borne fruit.

Now all we needed to do was make it back.

This became an annual event at Ixopo High for the next five years - and I never lost or killed a single child - trust me. Gareth joined us in 1993, riding an old XR200 and, at 13, I have no doubt is the youngest person ever to have ridden a motorcycle up Southern Africa's highest mountain.

But before I got sidetracked by this bit of nostalgia, I was admitting to having once before received sponsorship. I thought I'd try to get some free goodies for my pupils (and myself, obviously). In the end we were given a new rear knobbly each (made by some obscure Korean company), and I was given a pair of Yoko enduro trousers - obviously rejects because they had the "YOKO" stitched on the wrong way round.

It didn't worry me and the tyres worked a treat!

Nearly there!

Fitted new knobblies to both bikes, front and back. They look great and should help with what the mountains have to throw at us in a few weeks' time. We will be crating the bikes for the flight to Almaty one week from tomorrow, so need to have everything ready and packed for then.

Gareth informed me that our return trip through Kazakhstan is going to be longer than it already is: The Ruskies have leased (claimed) a large tract of central Kazakhstan for their space programme and have declared it part of Russia. Evidently we need a visa to enter and, only having a single entry visa for Russia in our passports, we will have to take the long way round, adding significantly to the distance of our return trip. Also, it seems that the permits we have for the border regions of Kazakhstan and Tajikistan do not cover all the more sensitive areas - just the very parts we want to travel through. One thread on the Internet offers various advice by travellers who have been there: *Just go and, when caught, pay the fine... Go and when turned back, obey and then find a track around.*

Evidently there are lots of small tracks through the mountains; the only problem is getting lost. Acquiring the correct stamps, according to those in the know, will require a great deal of contortion, hoop jumping and, the main problem - time. More than we've got.

Back to the usual stand-by: just go there, suck it and see.

Just a few days to go now. Gareth and I rode the bikes to a nondescript warehouse in the south west suburbs of Manchester just before midday to be met by a helpful representative of James Cargo Services Ltd, ready to assist with the crating of the bikes. I had spent the last two days doing a final pack, sorting out things that had to go on the bike and those that would come with us on the plane.

I'd changed £1000 into US dollars, crisp new 50, 20 and 1 dollar notes and had, as has been my practice for all of my trips, divided the money into equal piles and wrapped them in gaffer-taped plastic. These I stow, cunningly taped onto inside plastic surfaces on the bike, distributed around my clothing and hidden in my luggage. So, if I'm robbed or if the bike crashes and burns or is stolen or if one of my panniers or bags is removed, only a portion of the money will disappear. The notes need to be new, evidentially, because old or tatty ones are not accepted or will attract a lower exchange rate. Large notes for normal exchange, small for "gifts" or whatever.

(At the last minute, however, we were advised not to have any money on the bikes because the Kazakhstan customs officers might just find them and object so I unscrewed the side covers and stripped out my carefully hidden dollars. I'll replace them when we get the bikes out of customs.)

Other than that, a basic set of tools and spares were stowed away, one change of clothes, some emergency food in case we are stuck somewhere in the mountains for a while, maps and documents, camping gear. All packed and triple strapped down, all ship-shape.

Gareth, who always seems to manage to take less than me (or just packs it better) had fitted his Ebay-purchased soft panniers to the sides of his KTM, having had to construct aluminium brackets to keep them away from the exhausts. Fitted with catalytic converters, these generate a tremendous amount of heat and will melt anything combustible that comes near them. Even after the short ride to James Cargo, a loose strap had touched one of the pipes and melted into a black goo. I have a feeling he's going to have a problem or two with this on the trip. Not enough testing to see whether the luggage will stay in place over rough terrain. But his method is light and simple, unlike the rigid frame I have built to hold my panniers and fuel container. We are carrying an extra nineteen litres of petrol between us in three Rotax containers which should be enough.

So, after some initial chit-chat - James is a biker himself - we got down to business. The cargo company collects used crates from BMW after they have imported their bikes and, for a small donation to charity for each crate, re-uses them to move bikes around the world. A most cost-effective and efficient plan. We started with my KLE, removing the front wheel and mounting the spindle in a small, wooden cradle on the bottom frame of the crate, then strapping it down securely. Then I removed my panniers which were bubble-wrapped, as was my front wheel, and these were strapped alongside the engine. James reminded us to reduce the pressure in our tyres by about a half so they didn't explode at altitude, which we did. Then repeat for Gareth's bike, removing his screen and rear view mirrors as well because of the added height of the KTM. We left James to nail on the sides and top of the crates and headed home, hoping we would see our bikes in Almaty, safe and whole, in a few days' time.

The final days before lift-off I spent listening to my Russian language tapes, printing off a number of family pics as gifts/conversation pieces for when we stay with local families in their yurts and running off a number of mock "official" copies of our passports, with the correct address of the British Consulate in London, "Certified a true copy" declaration (well, it *is)* and a suitably (I thought) authentic signature. Hopefully we will be able to palm these off to any soldiers/policemen/corrupt officials who might be tempted to confiscate our passports and hold them against the provision of a bribe. That and my copied and laminated driver's licence and expired credit card, all held in a false wallet, might get us out of a few problems - but probably not. We shall see.

Ready to go. Bikes should be waiting for us in Almaty as I type this.

Sadly, the situation in eastern Ukraine is worsening. Just this morning, the day before we leave, pro-Russian separatists shot down an Antonov Il-76 transport plane carrying 49 soldiers - all killed. Such a tragedy.

We need to work out a few possible alternative routes home in case the whole of eastern Ukraine is blocked by fighting.

So, the adventure begins...

Touch-down in Kazakhstan - The adventure begins

A dull, wet and depressing Almaty greeted us wanly after our artificially contracted flight, travelling as we were against the thrust of the earth's spin. Peering with sleep-deprived eyes out the aircraft window, Gareth pointed out a gun-toting Kazakh border official standing on the wet concourse and said with a laugh, "He's trying to stop any of us getting away!"

In the tunnel from the aircraft into the terminal building, another guard eyed us suspiciously from behind the high Soviet-style peak of his cap. He looked strangely like a slightly thinner Vladimir Putin on a clandestine visit to check out his old republics and see how they were doing.

Or whether any needed invading.

We passed through customs without incident and then changed some money - $100 each - just to get us going and to know what the exchange rate was so we wouldn't get ripped off later on the street. A wise move, as it turned out.

A taxi tout took us in hand, literally, and led us to a waiting vehicle outside. The driver was silent and sullen and it was clear he had no meter. Without communicating, both Gareth and I knew this was going to end in a fight. We sat back, still thick-headed from jet-lag, music from a local radio station assaulting our ears, and waited for the attempted rip-off to begin.

A short ten ks from the airport we were dropped off at our hotel and our surly driver, without so much as a blush, stuck out his hand and demanded T19,000 - over $100 - for the ten minute trip.

But he wasn't dealing with novices here. Seasoned travellers we! First, we knew the exchange rate so could convert his price into dollars and be one step ahead of his game.

We told him to push off.

But our guy was clever; he'd obviously done this before and had come prepared, producing a laminated card with the prices neatly typed out. He stuck his finger on a line which clearly said:

"Airport to crummy hotel: T19,000 - special tourist rip-off price."

I laughed in his face and told him I was calling the police.

He phoned his supervisor and passed the mobile to me. A voice (speaking good English) assured me that it was the correct price.

I laughed at him too, "Yeah, right!"

He quickly offered T17,000 and then T15,000.

I told *him* I was calling the police and gave the phone back to our driver who pointed at his watch and muttered.

We ignored him.

Leaving him standing next to his car, we both headed off to look for someone local and authoritative to refute the charge. I spoke to two parking attendants with limited English while Gareth entered the hotel, emerging a few minutes later with a grin on his face and holding T3000 which he flung onto the front seat of the taxi with a contemptuous flourish.

We took our bags and left.

One-nil to us.

Just thirty minutes into Kazakhstan and we were already being scammed...

Later we met Dorien, our fixer who would spend all day with us getting the bikes out of customs. Heavily acne-scarred and with slightly Mongoloid features, he spoke excellent English and led us through the bewildering formalities of releasing the bikes with an efficiency bred from long experience. Bundled into his car, we set off on what seemed like a real-life episode of *Russian Drivers' Worst Just Misses* on You-Tube. He had a dashboard camera pointing at the road ahead, which I considered ominous. He told us it was to gather evidence in case someone drove into him - which, judging from the drivers with whom we were jostling, was a distinct possibility. After driving like an idiot across the suburbs of Almaty, he turned to us and said, shaking his head sadly, "When you get into Kyrgyzstan, watch out - they drive like idiots!"

He told us he rode a Harley and, before this job, worked in the Kazakh oil fields where temperatures in winter can fall to -50 degrees C and the roads after each winter look like a bomb site because of corruption and poor workmanship. Negotiating a particularly bad section of road, he told us that he'd smashed his front wheel the previous week hitting a deep pothole. The speed limit on main roads is 100kph but, really, he laughed, this was not necessary because the roads are so bad that you would be mad to drive any faster than that.

The main road to the airport, though, was in good condition, clean and well maintained. Gangs of workers were sweeping the edges while others with hose pipes washed it down. I was impressed - until Dorien wryly informed us that this was the road the president used on his way to the airport and it was kept clean and *washed* just for him.

We passed through neighbourhoods with buildings of brutally utilitarian design, graced with peeling paint, flaking plaster, exposed wires and ill-fitting joints, finally arriving at the customs sheds, a bare and Spartan place with some offices housed in what looked like reject shipping containers. And, for the rest of the day we had to contend with hours of typical ex-Soviet bureaucracy, slow, methodical, repetitive, frustrating. The officials were always polite, but each step in the process was conducted with ponderous formality, official stamps accumulating on every page of our documentation, tracking from one office to another across dusty, heat-soaked courtyards, buying warm drinks from a damaged vending machine and using a toilet with no toilet paper: queue and wait, queue and wait under the burning Kazakh sun. Throughout the day, Dorien ushered us through the whole convoluted process with a resigned patience and unflagging enthusiasm.

Finally, as the afternoon waned, he flourished a sheaf of papers and declared that we were done. Trust me, at $120 for his efforts, Dorien was cheap.

Now, getting the bikes out of the customs warehouse was not as simple a task as it might seem. First, we had to hire a truck driver - there were trucks of varying sizes parked outside - and Dorien selected one. Our driver sported a baseball cap, yellow dark glasses and two gold-capped front teeth.

He asked us where we were going and we told him.

"Afghanistan?" he asked tentatively.

We shook our heads.

"Not good," he warned, making machine gun noises whilst holding an imaginary AK in front of his chest. Then his mobile rang; his ring tone, appropriately, was the sound of a Kalashnikov firing.

I placed my bag on the dashboard of his truck but he wagged a finger and warned, "Not good." He hid it in the foot well and locked the cab. Evidently even within the security of the customs enclosure things are not safe. Dorien told us that his rear-view mirrors had been stolen off his car a short while back and a friend had discovered one morning that both doors had been removed from his car.

To get our bikes out, the deal was this: We pay the driver $92 and he would drive through the gates, pick up the bikes and drive out again.

We paid.

An hour later a fork lift was procured from somewhere while we waited in the blazing sun; various bits of wood were acquired and the bikes manoeuvred, rather precariously, onto the truck which was driven the twenty metres out the gate and parked while we broke open the crates and man-handled our bikes off the back. No damage; all the bits where we had left them. Sweating profusely in the heat, we assembled the front wheels, attached our panniers and followed Dorien through the traffic back to our hotel.

We had our wheels...

Kyrgyzstan and corrupt border officials

The customs officer at the Kyrgyzstan border sat fatly in his chair and looked us over. He clutched our documents in his pudgy little hands. Then he leant forwards, tapped the papers with a fat finger and said, without a blush, "One hundred dollars."

Welcome to Kyrgyzstan!

It took us a while to pack up (how come there always seems to be more stuff to pack away in your panniers on the morning of the first day of a trip than there was when you stowed it all away neatly before the trip began?) and get out of the sprawling suburbs of Almaty, once the capital but now the commercial hub of Kazakhstan. Our first experience of riding through traffic in the oppressive low-altitude heat of a Central Asian summer was sobering and we suffered. The road east from Almaty towards Karakol on the eastern shore of Lake Ysyk-Kol was a patchwork of repairs but fortunately pothole free. Policemen were stationed outside every village, trapping. We rode circumspectly, wanting no further brushes with mendacious officialdom.

There comes a time on every journey when you can finally say, "It's started!" A trip like this doesn't begin when the bikes are finally released from the customs shed or when you load up and set off one hot morning through the snarl of hooting traffic and diesel fumes in some foreign city. It starts somewhere further out. The buildings fall away, the landscape opens up, trees replace concrete lamp posts, the horizon becomes visible. The increased speed cools your body; wide-open spaces gentle the spirit.

And suddenly the realisation comes: *It's begun!*

After six months of waiting and desultory preparation, we were finally on our way; at last we were riding in Kazakhstan. The mountains of the notorious Pamir knot awaited us just over *there!*

Herds of horses appeared, standing as still as the yellow-grassed plains which disappeared into the heat-haze of the horizon; birds of prey hung effortlessly, crucified on their outstretched wings, lifted by updrafts from the hot plains. For a hundred kilometres or more, the road was lined by avenues of trees, bowls painted white to the height of a man, masking the drab, flat monotony of the plains to the north.

Riding ahead of me, Gareth suddenly pointed to our right and there, through a gap in the avenue of trees, could be seen a range of snow-capped mountains I had not noticed before, masked as they were by the buildings and the dust and smog of Almaty, so high their snow-covered peaks could easily be confused with clouds. The Kungoy Ala-Too mountain range, over 4000m high and the first of many we would have to cross over the next few weeks. I felt a tightness in my chest at the thought of riding over those mountains and the ranges that followed, wave after knotted wave through into China, Pakistan, Afghanistan, Kyrgyzstan, Tajikistan... Their names would change - Pamir, Hindu Kush, Karakorum, Himilaya, Kunlun, Tian Shan - but, essentially, facing us was a continent-sized vortex of tectonic forces and colliding mountain ranges still rising from the Indian sub-continent ploughing its way into the Asian tectonic plate, a massive colliding that began millions of years ago.

Which explains the earthquakes, I suppose.

And the landslides...

About 140ks out of Almaty, just after the town of Shilik, the road turns south east and immediately begins to rise into the foothills of the Kungoy Ala-Too which form the border here between Kazakhstan and Kyrgyzstan. As if a switch had been turned, people and vegetation disappeared; we continued to ride through an isolated semi-desert landscape reminiscent of the American badlands, crossing the Kegen River that had cut deeply through the yellow sandstone of the mountains.

Then we were at the Kazakh border only to find that Gareth had lost the one piece of paper, many stamped and signed and stamped again, that Dorien warned us *never* - on pain of death - to lose because without it, the importation of the bike would not be valid and we would be seriously in the dwang; added to that, my document (that I had not lost) clearly stated that we would be leaving Kazakhstan at a different border crossing two days' ride to the west on the far side of Almaty.

Oops!

But the border official was almost avuncular in the kind way he dealt with us. "Do not be afraid," he reassured, and proceeded to dictate to Gareth a grovelling letter to the Chief of Immigration for the Almaty Region, a certain Mr Volkov, which Gareth wrote out and signed. This done, the kind man filled out another precious form for Gareth's bike, attached the necessary stamps and we were free to go.

Bless him.

Now we could enter Kyrgyzstan and be met by the pudgy customs official, our documents in his grubby hands, trying to extort $100 out of us.

We stared at him, feigning incomprehension, doing what we have learned to do over the years when scummy, corrupt officials try to bribe or scam us: look blank, act as if you don't understand and wait them out.

It works like this: If you let them know you know you're being scammed, it becomes a confrontation. They want money; you don't want to give them money - it's a clash of wills, a challenge to their authority. If you win, they lose face.

But if you act as if you *don't understand* then everything takes on a different complexion. There's no loss of face. Each time they ask for money, just be extra helpful, dig into your file of papers and offer them random things with eager cooperation: "Insurance - yes, of course I've got insurance. Would you like to see it? Here -"

Impassive, he tapped the forms and repeated, "One hundred dollars -"

"Oh, *paspirt* for the bikes - yes, got that - here -"

He stared at us with his little, avaricious, piggy eyes, waiting.

Getting bored, I asked him, "Can we have our documents, please?" and held out my hand.

He picked up a piece of paper, tore off a scrap and wrote *$10* on it, pushed it towards us and muttered, "Ten dollars - for document..." just in case we hadn't got the message.

I put on a fake embarrassed smile and handed him my whole wallet of documents - *take your pick*. "Sorry, I don't understand - you want *visa*?"

"Ten dollars -" he insisted, tapping the piece of paper.

In the end we just waited, staring at him. He probably knew we were playing our little game of deliberate incomprehension, but there wasn't much he could do about it.

Eventually I reached over and took the papers out of his hand, saying again, "Can we have our documents, please?"

He let them go and then, unaccountably, his whole demeanour changed, standing up to shake our hands and wish us goodbye in a most ingratiating manner.

Shortly after leaving the border we were flagged down by a policeman who also asked for money, muttering about some document. Once again we acted dumb and he gave up.

If, however, the extortion is obvious and can't be ignored or deliberately misunderstood, we have found the best solution is just to ask to see the paperwork, insist on a receipt for any payment made and wait. Never take out your wallet. Just remove your jacket, helmet and gloves, sit down on the side of the road, take out your water bottle and have a drink - make the message clear: *I can wait as long as you like, my friend, but I'm not giving you any money.* It usually works.

Lonely Planet has this to say about this aspect of the 'Stans: "Now that the long, unyielding arm of Russian law is no longer on the scene, corruption by officials and political turmoil are part of daily life."

Yes, so we had noticed.

The roads in Kyrgyzstan so far had varied between good tar and very rough dirt; if the dirt roads on a seemingly *main* road from the border to the town of Karakol were anything to go by, I felt, we were in for an interesting time when the road degenerated from bold red to black to a small dotted line on the map.

Finally, after a good day's ride, we found a small home-stay in the town of Karakol: cheap and cheerful, World Cup soccer on the telly, a bony dog chained to the gate as a perpetual guard (I gave him water and fed him all the left-over cheese from supper and he became my friend).

As evening cooled the air, following the smell of animal dung, I sneaked through a small side door to be confronted by another world, hidden away - a world which, I assume, existed before the concept of home-stays became an easy way for Kyrgyz families to make some extra money: in earthen pens, goats were tethered and a small vegetable garden flourished. It was like a mini farm tucked away behind the façade of the boarding house where their *real* life was lived when we were not there.

Lake Song-Kol

We rode on through dusty towns in states of dilapidation one would expect from an ex-Soviet era - wooden lamp posts leaned drunkenly, held up by concrete poles, rats' nests of wires hanging in the wind; sagging, blue-painted picket fences separated houses from dusty streets; rusted transformers balanced precariously on concrete pipes and piles of rubble, wires exposed for anyone who might be looking for a quick and certain suicide. But all this scrabbling poverty was redeemed by the cool avenues of tall, pale-trunked poplars lining the roads, muting the sparseness of life with green.

A road, patched and lumpy but serviceable, two hundred kilometres long, runs from Karakol to Balykchy, following the shore of lake Ysyk-Kol, blue-green and clear but later in the afternoon darkening to a dull grey as the clouds closed in and it began raining. At first the lake cannot be seen and the road follows the largely flat, 40km wide Karkara Valley floor between the parallel mountain ranges of the Kungoy Ala-Too and the Central Tian Shan, both snow-covered in places but the Tian Shan significantly higher, being snow-covered throughout the year. These were soon blotted out by lowering clouds so that only the foothills could be seen, made up of a bright yellow sandstone, deeply eroded. This wide valley straddles the Kazakh-Kyrgzystan border. Finally the road joins the lake which it follows closely for the next hundred or so kilometres.

Lake Ysyk-Kol ("Warm Lake") is significant in a number of ways: First, its size. At 170km long and 70km wide, it is the world's second largest alpine lake after Lake Titicaca in the Andes. Secondly, and of greater significance, is that it never freezes. This is because of its great depth, thermal activity and its slight salinity. A combination of its size and warmth has a moderating influence on the climate of the surrounding countryside and makes it an ideal holiday destination for those living in the sultry lowlands.

We finally left the lake and took a small road across a stark, arid plain before beginning to rise into the Central Tian Shan mountains. We passed Muslim cemeteries like miniature cities outside each village; women and children queuing with brightly-coloured plastic buckets at communal water spouts; massive, rusting monuments to fallen soldiers of the 1941-45 war, much neglected as so many ex-Soviet monuments are.

At midday we paused for lunch at a smoky shed on the side of the road and were introduced to *shaslik*, a staple throughout Central Asia and available pretty much anywhere. Just look for the blue, rising smoke and you'll find a rectangular metal *sashlik* burner, coals banked on one side, lumps of sheep threaded onto flat, metal skewers cooking, the vendor usually swathed in smoke as he tends to his meat. We came to enjoy the smoky flavour of this mutton and, unusually, found the meat remarkably tender.

At a low table across from us a large Kyrghz family noisily ate their meal, the men, dark-skinned and with flashing gold-capped teeth, washing down their *shaslik* with large goblets of vodka. As one does. We, being boring (and alive), drank black tea from small bowls. A confident, round-faced child of about five left the family group and sat at our table, staring at us as we ate.

Finally, as the afternoon waned and the road headed north-west towards Balykchy, we turned off onto a narrow road acting as a short cut onto the E125 south. Our aim was to find the turn-off to the high mountain lake of Song-Kol, remote and beautiful according to those in the know. After ninety kilometres we found the narrow dirt road which made its way towards the snow-covered Kalmak-Ashuu Pass and began the long climb. On the way we passed large herds of sheep and shaggy cattle, the herders beginning to favour traditional yurts instead of the usual square, brick-built houses.

And it was here that I saw it: The sun broke through the clouds and brushed the eroded mountain slopes with delicate shades of pink and mauve and yellow, darker where the rocks showed through, brilliant white above the snow line; and, in a surreal merging of reality and memory, I saw a green valley with small meandering stream, the pastel-shaded mountains disappearing into the distance where they merged with the sky, a gravel track twisting its slow way through. *This* was what I remember seeing in the original photograph Gareth sent me with his tantalizing comment, "Next year?" that had sown the seed for this trip.

Well, I thought, the next year is *now* and we are *here!* The mountains of my imagination had become real and we were riding through and over them, feeling the bare earth under our wheels, the air icy cold against our skin, and I was filled with a sense of unspeakable joy.

Having climbed above the snow line over the pass, the road dipped into a vast, shallow bowl, a col-like expanse at least twenty miles across and, at the centre, like a blue eye, lake Song-Kol, round and still, reflecting the surrounding mountains and the clouds above.

We made our way down to the lake then left the road to follow its edge for a few kilometres, the ground firm and undulating, and set up camp almost level with the water, the grass short and green and covered with yellow daisies. We erected our tents under a sky dramatic with white cumulus clouds while, behind us, a storm brewed over the mountains we had just crossed, the sky black and streaked with rain. Thunder rumbled, echoing around the col.

Other than that, the only sound was that of the wind.

As the sun set, a hard, biting cold entered our bones and I put on first one then a second layer of thermal underwear, my jumper and, finally, the inners from my riding gear and both pairs of socks. Perhaps a nice, hot cuppa would hit the spot, I thought, followed by a stew made from our emergency rations of salami and powdered soup? Mmmm!

Except it was then that Gareth discovered that he'd left the stove behind. To cut down on weight, we'd decided that we'd just bring the one so we now had two sets of pots, fuel - but no stove or wood. There was the occasional cow pat lying on the grass but they were all wet and unusable.

Bummer! It got even colder. I wished I'd packed a large bottle of Old Brown sherry or a cheeky red. Perhaps some *Wodka*?

Fortunately we had bought a few bits and pieces at the last village so we ate a rather piquant supper of cold salami, raw onion, cucumber and flat bread washed down with water.

But I wouldn't have wanted it any different.

A twelve-hour day

The yurt inside was as attractive and welcoming as the Kyrgyz pastoralist family had been outside.

As is the custom of hospitality in most remote and isolated parts of the world, the moment they saw us approaching, we were warmly greeted and invited into their yurt for a cup of tea. These open-hearted people always seem to give the impression that it is we who are conferring upon them an honour by our mere presence in their homes rather than the other way round; as we repeatedly found on the trip, the offer of a cup of tea never means just tea: always the best of their food, however simple, would be brought out and we would be urged to eat. How much we in the West can learn from their welcome and generosity.

Seeing the two yurts pitched on a grassy plain close to the lake just after we had set off on the long haul to Jalal-Abad the next morning, I decided to make a stop to confirm our direction (and, if I'm honest, because I hoped we might be invited in for a cup of tea). I was not disappointed. This was no tourist yurt designed for home-stays; it was just a normal Kyrgyz family - grandfather and grandmother, their son and his wife and four young children who occupied the yurt immediately alongside.

Inside, the yurt was surprisingly spacious, the floor covered with patterned carpets and sheep skins; the bedding - which seemed to consist of skin mats upon which a mattress of some kind was laid - had been raised and strapped against the side wall of the yurt, increasing the living space. Sparsely utilitarian yet comfortable, it was clear that nothing superfluous cluttered their lives. The sides and roof of the structure were held up with a light lattice of thin pieces of wood over which the heavy compressed hair "skin" was stretched and held in place with ropes. Against the wall on one side was a metal stove for cooking and heating, the chimney passing through a hole in the roof; alongside it stood a wooden barrel with protruding ladle full of sour milk. Soft sheep skins were provided for sitting on in front of a low table covered with a white cloth.

It became clear on this trip that people living in remote locations on the very edge of subsistence make use of whatever they can harvest from their flocks and their surroundings for food. What was placed before us seldom varied: usually bowls of thick cream, sour milk, cucumber and tomato, flat bread and black tea. In return, we always tried to leave some of our food to compensate them for their loss. I have no doubt they would have given us their last meal if need be and only once were we asked for payment - and that was from a shifty-eyed fat woman in a town who tried to rip us off.

While tea was being made, we conducted a fair conversation, exchanging names and addresses, expressing mutual admiration for Manchester United (although Gareth, who shows no interest in football at all, insisted he supported Man City). The grandfather, who did most of the talking, expressed sadness at the parlous state of the English football team and their chances in the World Cup, favouring, in his opinion, Spain and Italy. We established our knowledge of each others' countries' capital cities and we told them where we were headed next. That was about the extent of our chit-chat using sign language, facial expressions and our limited knowledge of English and Russian. But soon tea was produced followed by flat bread, a bowl of butter, the clotted cream, cucumber and sour milk; we were given forks and repeatedly urged to eat.

On our second fill of tea, Gareth said to me quietly how much he would like to photograph the family in their yurt but we agreed that it would be churlish to suggest it. By this time I had the youngest child - fat and rosy-cheeked (from all the cream, I would imagine) - sitting on my lap and I had given them a photograph of our family, including my wife, daughter and first granddaughter. This created a bond between the old man and me as he pointed to his four grandchildren with a gap-toothed grin. Then he made a camera-clicking gesture and insisted we take photographs of his family, which we did. As we have his address, we will send him copies when we get home - but whether they will reach him so far up in the mountains is another story.

The night camping by the side of Lake Song-Kol had been cold despite all my layers of clothing and I discovered, again, that the ageing process does not make sleeping on the ground any easier. My joints ached, my bones seemed more angular and my flesh less padded than I remembered. It was a long night.

But, as always, as soon as we were packed up and on the road, all the travails of the previous night evaporated. The road around Lake Song-Kol was motorcycle heaven: smooth and undulating, we were able to fly along at 70ks an hour, stopping only once (other than our yurt visit) at a washed away bridge where a truck had become stuck in the river crossing. We paused to watch the driver jack up the back wheels one at a time whilst standing in the river, and thrust lengths of cut saplings about the thickness of my arm, strapped together with rope, under the wheels. Finally, with a great billowing of diesel fumes, he accelerated clear and made it across to the other side.

Reluctantly, after an hour's riding, we left the lake and began climbing the first of many passes that were to confront us during the day, all between 2,500 and 3,300m high. The road, at first, was good but going was slow because of the many switchbacks and the loose gravel that made riding a challenge, especially on the tight corners. I had by then become used to the odd sensation of the laden bike floating and drifting about on gravel roads, so far - long may it stay this way - under control.

Near midday we descended into a wide, high valley, hot and dry, the sun beating down on us in our heavy riding gear despite the moderating effect of altitude. The road turned nasty, rocky and corrugated. But on either side of the valley the high mountain ranges were beautiful in their starkness. Consisting of a soft, eroded sandstone, these mountains are a harsh yellow in the heat of the day but, as evening sets in and the day begins to cool, the sandstone mutes and is shadowed with blues and pinks, mauves and lilacs, and the land takes on a naked remoteness, nuanced and beautiful.

We rode hard for nearly twelve hours that day, stopping briefly to top up our tanks with petrol from our spare containers, eat *shashlik* from a roadside stall and chat with a pair of English cyclists who were seven months into a trip from the UK to Bankok. They had been *pushing* their loaded bikes up a particularly long pass for two days, their tyres down to the canvass and shredded from the rocks.

Respect.

Blokes like that put our trip into perspective: they're on a *real* adventure; we're just playing games.

Hoping to reach Jalal-Abad by evening, we finally struck tar in the town of Kazarman as the sun sank low over the surrounding mountains. One hundred and fifty kilometres to go. But the tar lasted only about five kilometres before we were faced with the worst road we had faced all day (or the best, depending on your perspective). In a few places landslides had covered the track but graders had cut a way through, one still working as we passed. Rain was falling high in the mountains ahead, the sky black and glowing intermittently with lightning flashes. In some places, the road itself had become a river and we splashed our way upward into the mountains, rain-dark and threatening, stopping half way up to zip our jackets as hail pounded down.

Kaldama Pass, 3062m, was snow-covered as we neared the top, banks of old snow twenty foot high on the lee of the road, their bases hollowed out and leached as the melt water poured from beneath them and joined the run-off from the storm. From the top of the pass it seemed as if the whole of Kyrgyzstan was laid out at our feet, range after distant range of mountains dipping to the horizon in all directions, the road writhing and twisting up one side and repeating its meandering path all the way into the dry heat of the next valley.

We pressed on, desperate for a shop so we could get something to drink, not having consumed anything but water all day.

Finally, now after six, we reached the tar and made our way through Jalal-Abad and on to the town of Osh, having been in the saddle, with various short stops, for twelve long hours. We found a humble home-stay where the matriarch, a short, plump, olive-skinned woman, her head covered by a severe scarf tied under her chin, loose gown over a plain dress, took control of us. Her hands were thick, the skin coarse and rough from work, her face lined, severe and intimidating but when she smiled it could break your heart. Watching her, I had this vision of her being prepared to kill for those she loved and to die for her beliefs; there was that kind of strength about her. As soon as we arrived, the matriarch bossed us about as if she were our mother. We were ordered to wear shoes around the compound (but not when eating); I was looked at disapprovingly when I removed my dusty riding boots and walked inside still wearing my sweat-damp socks. Her daughter immediately took a cloth and wiped the floor after me. I felt duly chastened. We were instructed where to put our dusty kit (a gnarled finger pointing at the *exact* spot), told what we were having for supper and informed that it would be ready when it was ready.

But she, her daughter and three granddaughters ran a tight ship - spotlessly clean, the rough concrete courtyard swept and sprinkled with water to quell the dust and cool the air. The long-drop toilet, too, was spotless and odour-free.

Our meal was tastefully served and, while we ate, I watched her three little grandchildren consume their meal unsupervised at a separate table just across the courtyard from us, and their manners were impeccable. After dinner, the eldest - she must have been about seven - settled down to do her homework of carefully copied handwriting exercises.

Later, surreptitiously watching the young grandchildren and their delicate-boned mother wash at the courtyard tap while writing up my journal, I became aware of what a dignified people the Kyrgyzs are: gentle, reserved, generous, always respecting one's personal space.

Unloading the bikes that evening, Gareth discovered a tear in the side wall of his rear tyre. We didn't have a gaiter so decided to just keep an eye on it. Although there were no other visible signs of distress, we knew that the bikes were taking a beating. We both acknowledged that we were probably punishing the bikes by riding a little too fast and hard, considering the loads we were carrying and the condition of the roads. Many times on this trip we wondered how any loaded bike can take the beating that ours took day after day and still hold together - a credit to the designers and manufacturers.

"Into Tajikistan tomorrow," I wrote in my journal that night, *"but we will have to take a long detour because the main road cuts through a protruding tongue of Kazakhstan and we only have a dual-entry visa."*

"One of the passes we will cross," I continued in a fit of hubris, as things turned out, *"is a thousand metres higher than the highest we have crossed so far. Should be interesting..."*

Landslide

You can control the roads but you can't do much about landslides (well, you can if you're Swiss).

We were *nearly* there, just twenty kilometres to go; just a few more corners and we'd be at the top of Taldyk Pass. We had reached 3,350m and the highest point of the pass is 3,615.

Just another 265 metres to go...

Well, as you know from my introduction, it wasn't to be.

The day went like this:

Saying farewell to our hosts, we set off towards the Tajik border. Only after we'd been going for a while did I realise that we were actually travelling on the legendary Silk Road. Now I realise admitting this makes me look just a little like a cretin but, ah, well - this is an honest account.

It's like when you haven't seen someone for many years you assume that, even though a decade or two might have passed, they will look exactly the same as when you last saw them - so with the Silk Road highway. For so long we have been told about how this remote and perilous route from China to the West through the mountains and deserts of the 'Stans was used by traders for thousands of years; so, naturally, one expects it to be *old,* that it will have still the deep footprints of camels pressed into the mud and snow of high mountain passes; one imagines narrow, scree-covered dirt tracks making their way through steep valleys, ancient mountains hanging over the road, a perilous place, remote and wild and dangerous. I imagined it as it probably was when Marco Polo made his way through this region so long ago.

And so it came as something of a surprise to realise that, over the last thousand or so years, things have changed: tar roads have been invented and, yes, indeedy, Sir, this amazing technology has even reached the 'Stans.

In fact, the Silk Road we rode along soon after leaving Osh was as good as any you could find in the UK, wide and smooth and well made. And after the previous day's long, bruising twelve hours over passes too many to count and roads that beat us and the bikes unmercifully, it was a pleasure to have a "rest day", riding in bright sunshine over a tar road any First World country would be proud of (well, except for the numerous stray cows meandering into the centre of the road to meditate, huge herds of ragged sheep driven by Kyrgyz herders on horseback who seemed to imply by their lack of concern for passing vehicles that they have *always* herded their animals along this track, following the river valley, long before a road was even thought of, thank you, and that's the way it's going to stay; and massive chunks excised out of the road for repair and replacement, only some of which were marked by barriers of rocks placed across the road.)

So we rode, relaxed and carefree, for about two hundred kilometres along the legendary Silk Road that made its way through green valleys cultivated with wheat and rice and maize, the mountains snow-topped, high and blue on either side, cumulus clouds massing above us as the hot, humid air of the lowlands rose and cooled. And as I rode along the civilizing strip of tar which seemed to have tamed this part of Kyrgyzstan, I allowed my mind to drift back to the days when the Silk Road was being used as the only viable route through this forbidding cluster, this "tangled knot" of mountains ranged across the centre of Asia, of camel trains hundreds long, making their slow way between hunched mountains, slipping on the vast bands of scree still clustered on the lower slopes, inching along narrow, meandering paths clinging to the banks of the same turbulent, loess-yellow river we were riding alongside at that moment. I imagined their fear of avalanches that have been known to wipe out entire camel trains, of attacks from unfriendly tribes through whose territory they had to make their way. These were the *same* mountains that looked down on them, the same rivers that flowed past them, at whose mud-frothed banks their camels and sheep and horses drank.

But that was a long time ago...

This was now and, so far, it had been a relaxing day's ride; no pressure; middling distance to cover, all on good tar.

And that's what caused the problem.

Because of the heat and the distance we needed to travel, sometimes we didn't bother with a midday meal - just a Coke or a cuppa from some roadside stall or eating house along the way. But on that day we had time. It was a day to relax. So I suggested we pause for a meal.

Which we did.

And there's the rub.

If we had just carried on riding, we would have made it across the pass before the landslide blocked the road; Gareth wouldn't have fallen ill from some dodgy road-kill meat we had for lunch.

We would have been in Tajikistan the next day.

But we weren't.

As we started up the long Taldyk Pass, the highest we had yet faced, dark clouds were massing ahead, blotting out the mountains with a grey smudge of rain. We stopped to zip up our riding gear, knowing we were going to get soaked. The rain started as soon as we began the switchbacks of the pass proper and, as we neared the top, it began to snow.

But it was OK - we only had twenty kilometres to go, only another few hundred metres of altitude, and then Sary Tash: hot shower, clean clothes, cold beer - the things that, at the end of a long day's ride, make life worthwhile.

And then we rounded a tight corner and saw the cars - just three of them - stopped in the middle of the road. Ahead, a massive chunk of mountain had broken away and slid into a cutting, filling it to the height of about eight metres at its lowest point. The entire cutting - through which we had to make our way - had been filled with thousands of tons of rock.

There was no way round - it was a *cutting*; mountains on both sides.

I rode my bike reasonably close to have a look-see. Some men, who had got out of their cars, shouted at me, pointing up at the raw mountainside and waving me back just as another section of mountain collapsed and came tumbling into the already half-filled cutting.

Clearly, it had only just happened - just a few minutes before we had arrived. The air was still full of the dank, mouldy smell of newly-disturbed earth and while we watched, more small rocks loosened and tumbled down.

There was a rawness about the scene: snow and rain falling about us, the rank smell of earth, the soughing of the wind, rocks loosening and tumbling down a ripped, newly-exposed rock-face. Suddenly the tar road we were standing didn't seem quite so civilizing any more.

We stood about, at a loss for what to do. Incongruously, an old man wearing a hi-viz jacket and clutching a spade - he must have been in one of the cars - stood looking forlornly at the pile of rock, big enough to fill a cathedral, as if wondering where to start.

It was obvious even to an optimist that no one was going to get any further on this road for a v-e-r-y l-o-n-g time.

Weeks?

So much for Sary Tash and my hot shower, clean clothes and cold beer. So much for Tajikistan and the Palmir Highway the next day...

The rain started to fall harder, icy with snow. We were freezing and Gareth was clearly ill. All he wanted to do was lie down and die.

We looked at the map - on the side of the road, in the rain.

Was there a way round?

Gareth did manage to pick out a small dotted line on the map some three hundred or so kilometres to the south and east that seemed to head in the right direction but he was feeling so ill that we needed to get off the mountain and out of the snow and rain as quickly as possible. Despite having ridden most of the day, the closest town was one hundred and forty kilometres away so, reluctantly, we turned the bikes around and set off down the pass again, heading for Osh where, eventually, we booked into a hostel.

Over supper we discussed our options.

Option A: Attempt this track over the mountains marked with a faint dotted line (Eski-Nookat - Papan - Sary-Mogol - Sary-Tash), 150ks long, so small you could hardly see it on the map - described in the Legend as: *Track (seasonal)*. This made it even more insignificant than the roads marked with a thin straight line (Tertiary Road) and a thicker hyphenated line (Other Road);

Or, Option B: Take the only other significant road into Tajikistan via Dushanbe, a deviation of some two thousand kilometres and (as it turned out) five days' hard travel before we struck the Pamir Highway again.

Later that evening we met David, an Auzzie biker on his way home via India and Malaysia. He was planning to meet some biker friends the next day who were on the *other* side of Sary Tash. It wasn't going to happen. We suggested that he contact them and tell them about the track we had found - maybe they could use it to get round the rock fall. After all, they'd be going *down* the pass instead of up.

"No, they wouldn't do that," David replied, looking at us as if we were mad.

That night, Gareth and I made our decision: Option A. We *had* to attempt the small track.

And so it was with a certain degree of excitement tinged with trepidation that I retired to bed that night. In the pit of my stomach, though, I knew that there was no way we were going to make it over those mountains. With a modern road crossing the Taldyk Pass just a few hundred kilometres away, why would *anyone* be stupid enough to attempt a pass on a dirt track? It had to be little used and, therefore, unmaintained. It would be snow-covered because of the altitude and muddy from the rains. It had to be *very* steep as it neared the top and clawed its way over the high peaks. How would we cope with heavily loaded bikes?

But we had to give it a try. And, anyway, it's attempts like these that become the stuff of memories...

The small dotted line

Let's be blunt here: this is not a *normal* country.

I'm not being derogatory - just stating a fact.

When you live in a normal country - like Britain, for example (although some, I'm sure, would question that) - you say to your spouse, "Let's go to Paris this weekend!" (not that I do that sort of thing often - well, let's be honest, never - it's just an example) - and you do. Or you might say, "Let's take a drive up to Scotland this summer!" - and you do.

That's what happens in normal countries.

But not here. Not in Kyrgyzstan.

Gareth and I want to travel to Tajikistan. There is only one road from Kyrgyzstan into Tajikistan from the north - via Sary Tash - unless you have a visa for Turkmenistan because, in its wisdom, when Russia created the 'Stans, it was as if some *Wodka*-addled general waved a drunken finger about on the map randomly between gulps, leaving small bits of one country isolated inside the borders of another like children left behind after a party, and long bits of one country protruding somewhat intrusively into their neighbour's territory like accusing fingers, often - quite unaccountability - crossing major roads in the process so everyone has to have a visa or stop to show their documentation at a hundred niggling little border crossings. Almost as if the Russians were playing their own little game called: How to annoy and inconvenience your neighbours and make them miserable.

(We actually discovered, after much asking and detailed explanations, in Russian that we only partially understood, that there *was* a way through. But that came later.)

So, it was the small dotted line, the *"Track (seasonal)"*, that we had to attempt. Ominously, we noticed that this track (I won't dignify it with the term "road") was not even marked on one of our maps. The night before, Gareth had checked on his GPS and found the track *was* there but only partially recorded. He also managed to get a satellite image on our Auzzie friend's phone; the photograph from space showed a track of sorts, but when zoomed in, the definition was so poor it gave no indication of its condition or even if it went the whole way over the mountains to the other side.

But something *was* there. The only solution was to go and have a look - which is what we did.

We got away early because we knew, deep down, that it was unlikely we would make it; we needed to give ourselves time to back track before darkness set in. Furthermore, the going up these rough, high tracks is painfully slow and often in the afternoon there is rain and we didn't relish trying to negotiate steep, wet rocks on loaded bikes.

At Kyzyl-Kyya we filled up our tanks and one spare Rotax container, just in case, and set off. At the garage (I use that term circumspectly because, off the beaten track in the 'Stans, you are more likely to have your tank filled with a bucket scooped out of a 44-gallon drum locked away in a dusty shed) Gareth looked up from his GPS and informed me, "Twenty kilometres and the map runs out..."

No more data. We would be on our own, half way up a scary range of mountains, with no GPS, a dodgy map and the track.

Later, when the GPS data *did* run out, our actual track was still being recorded so Gareth was able to keep us headed in the right direction, rather cleverly, I thought, by matching the scale of the GPS to that of the one map that showed the dotted line, looking at our back-track and matching the shape of our route to that on the map. In this way, at one point he noticed we were heading up a steep-sided valley in the wrong direction towards purple, snow-capped mountains that rose so high ahead of us that we had to crane our necks to see over the top of them. We back-tracked, found where we'd taken the wrong turn and carried on heading south along a stony track that followed the path of a fast-flowing river, turbulent with snow-melt, boiling and churning its way some distance below us.

The sun beat down on us from a cloudless sky. At least it wasn't going to rain - just yet, I thought. At times, when I could chance taking my eyes off the road, I looked up at the mountains ahead that barred our way and I could count *five* consecutive ranges, like massive waves in a turbulent sea, each higher and more hazed with blue than the next, the final mountain covered with snow and completely dominating the horizon. And, although both Gareth and I had known, ever since we first saw this tiny dotted line on the map, that our chances of making it were slim, I knew then for certain that this attempt was going to end in failure. The mountains were just too high; there were too many of them; the track, already rough, potholed and very stony, was bound to deteriorate and we hadn't even entered the foothills of the first range.

I had woken a few times the previous night, aware of a feeling of trepidation about the day ahead, that empty tightness in the stomach that speaks of fear or excitement (or maybe a bit of both). Off the main roads, little care is given to maintenance so that the roughness of the track becomes damaging to body and machine. But this was going to be altogether different and, as I rode, I found myself muttering, *"Whooo! Whooo!"* into my helmet, totally cowed by the enormity of the mountain ranges in front of us.

At the first army checkpoint behind a high, gaited fence, our papers were scrutinized by a young soldier with a firearm slung over his shoulder. The "office" was a converted metal container. There was an army 4X4 parked out back, the track ahead still had signs of tyre marks and the soldiers didn't laugh in our faces when we showed them on the map where we intended to go, so, momentarily, my hopes rose.

If a 4X4 had made it to this point, maybe others had made it right over the top and, if they could do it, surely we could too?

Papers checked and the gate opened to let us through, we pressed on along a stony track that quickly narrowed and became steeper. We had to battle our way through large herds of horses and sheep making their ponderous way up the pass, a rock wall on one side and a steep drop-off into the river on the other; often we had to push and nudge the sheep out of the way with our front wheels as we walked the bikes up the steep track, riding the clutch and pushing sheep aside with our knees. The horses, being more intelligent and skittish, made way for us; and the Kyrgyz drovers, usually two or three on horseback accompanied by a few large, ragged dogs and a donkey carrying their belongings, largely tolerated our presence with an ageless phlegmatism. The dogs were less happy to see us and eyed us warily as we passed.

About half an hour later a metal pole across the track signalled the second army checkpoint. In a single-roomed building were soldiers and a bed. One was asleep and roused himself drowsily to speak to us. He checked our papers, asked us where we were going and then insisted, *"Daroga nyet!"*, crossing his forearms in front of his chest and shaking his head.

The pass was closed. We weren't going to get through.

Not willing to give up until we were forced to, we persevered, showing the soldier the track we originally intended to take and indicating, with the same crossed-arms gesture, that the Sary-Tash road was blocked.

He demonstrated by holding his knees together and pushing with ski poles that it was snow that was blocking the pass, not him.

But we still wanted to see for ourselves, make it up as far as we could, at least demonstrate to ourselves that we'd done all we could. Eventually he filled our details into his register and raised the barrier to allow us through; we continued on up a track that grew still narrower and more covered with rocks that had tumbled from the steep mountain slopes all about us.

Perhaps there was still an infinitesimal flicker of hope that we might find a way through, snow or not, I can't remember. I think so, especially when we saw marks on the track indicating that, at some time in the past, a vehicle *had* travelled this way. Maybe it had made it all the way to the top.

Then we started coming across what was eventually to be our nemesis: scree. Tumbling and rolling down mountain slopes thousands of feet high, there is simply no stopping this constant fall of dislodged stones and rocks. It flows like water, collecting at the base of every mountain and, as roads in this place tend to follow river valleys, the scree slopes, over time, just flow over the road and cascade into the river on the other side. At first they were fairly small and we were able to take them at a run, as you would the low tongues of a dune. On some of the steeper slopes fallen rocks covered the track; there was no way round them and you couldn't stop so we just had to hit them and grimace at the noises of rocks hitting the bash plate and chassis of the bikes.

Then we came upon the third and final army checkpoint. And here the tracks ended. No vehicle had travelled further than this that we could see.

We made our way across a rickety bridge, rotten wooden slats through which the river could be seen tumbling its way down the mountainside, and approached a square building, table and benches outside under a large tree, shirtless soldiers playing soccer in the heat. The officer in charge welcomed us to his barren outpost and listened politely as we explained what we proposed to do, showing him the track on our map. But he shook his head. We could not proceed - but this time he didn't mention snow. Using gestures and the Russian we could understand, one of the soldiers explained that just eight kilometres from the checkpoint the track was blocked and we would only be able to proceed on foot or on horseback.

And a short while later we realised he was right.

Again we prevailed upon them to allow us through so we could see for ourselves and we pushed on along an even steeper, narrower track, jostling once again with herds of sheep and horses plodding their way up the pass with their herders on horseback guiding them. It was very hot and the bikes were overheating. So were we. We struggled on through breathtaking scenery, always the mountain barrier high and implacable in front of us, until, almost exactly eight kilometres from the military checkpoint, just as the soldier had predicted, our attempt ended.

I was in front at the time and saw too late that the road ahead, at the top of a steep incline, was completely covered with a thick, sloping layer of scree. I slowed briefly to work out a route across but the moment I accelerated again, the rear wheel immediately dug into the loose stones. I managed to get going again, hit the scree slope as hard as I could and bogged down again. A metre to my left dislodged rocks dropped off into the river fifty foot below. I tried once more to get moving but, the moment my rear wheel began to turn, it slipped sideways closer to the drop.

I didn't dare move. If I'd dropped the bike to the left, I'd have gone over the side and tumbled into the river, deep and turbulent, pale brown from snow-melt and eroded loess. While I waited, more scree slid down the mountain and pooled like water around my wheels and feet, starting to cover them. Fortunately I wasn't riding alone and soon Gareth had made his way up to me (but not before laughing and taking photographs -

as befits the actions of a solicitous son). Together, spinning the back wheel and both pushing, one on each side of the bike, we made it through to firm track on the other side.

Then it was Gareth's turn. He decided to power his way across at speed to stop the back wheel digging in and he began his run up the steep slope. Afterwards he told me what happened: first he missed a gear and couldn't get the run-up he wanted; but then his front wheel hit a rock which nudged him towards the edge and the river far below. He did the only thing he could to prevent himself going over: drop the big KTM in the middle of the scree bank.

So now it was my turn to laugh and take photos!

It was impossible for just the two of us to get the heavily-laden KTM across the scree so we unloaded it, dragged it on its side further away from the edge and, again both pushing and accelerating, made it across.

We could see that the track continued on its way up the mountain but we both realised it was the end. Clearly this was a track used by drovers taking their animals across the pass and not intended for vehicles. We hadn't even climbed a third of the three thousand or so metres that lay ahead of us and already we were struggling.

And so, thirty kilometres from the top - as the crow flies - our attempt came to an abrupt end.

I unloaded my bike, turned it and made my way gingerly across the scree, keeping well away from the drop-off into the river below; Gareth took it at pace and, going down hill, made it across easily. We loaded up again and began to retrace our steps, stopping to share lunch with the soldiers at the third checkpoint who smiled wryly when they saw us returning. They made us tea and gave us a loaf of flatbread and we spent a pleasant half hour with them in their Spartan, isolated outpost high in this desolate but beautiful place.

Concerned now that we were completely blocked from getting into Tajikistan - the Sary-Tash road blocked by a major landslide; the Dushanbe route blocked by our lack of a visa for Turkmenistan - Gareth took out our map and showed the soldiers where we wanted to go. One pointed out a small road that seemed to skirt around an isolated enclave of Turkmenistan and make it through. He seemed to be implying that there *was* a way round. Our hopes rose: we might still be able to do it.

Exhausted now from the effort of riding this track for hours and the enervating heat, I took a fall on the way down the pass which, while insignificant in terms of its damage to the bike and me, could have been serious. When riding a track littered with rocks of all sizes, it is simply impossible to miss them all. In places the whole road is made up of rocks, fist- to football-sized, and you just have to ride through and over them as best you can to get through. There's no alternative. You try to miss the larger ones but sometimes a brief loss of concentration and you hit a big one. Depending on where you hit a rock will determine what effect it has on the bike; if you're lucky and hit it square, you can just bash straight over it. But if you hit it at an angle it can shove you abruptly to one side. On a wide road this is not much of a problem; you just steer yourself upright again and carry on, telling yourself to miss the bloody rock next time. But when you're on a narrow track with no barrier of any kind, you just don't have the space - or time - to right the bike. Once you are leaning you have, of necessity, to travel a certain distance before you can get the bike to lean and turn in the opposite direction. And if that distance is occupied by air 30m above a river, there's little you can do but drop the bike and hope it stops sliding before it reaches the edge. The brakes won't stop it on a gravel surface and, if it's going to go over a cliff, I'd rather be lying on the road instead of sitting on the seat.

And, just like Gareth on the scree slope, my front wheel hit a large rock and it pushed me straight at the edge. No barrier, just the river a hundred foot down. So I dropped the bike. It was an automatic, instinctive action and it saved me. Fortunately I wasn't going fast so the bike and I slid to a stop just a foot from the edge. No damage. Realising I was no longer behind him, Gareth soon returned and helped me lift the bike (it was just too close to the edge for me to risk it on my own) and we continued on our way. But that near miss gave me some troubled nights for the next week or so.

On the way down we came across more herds of sheep and horses plodding their way up the narrow track. A herder on foot flagged me down making drinking gestures with his hand. Feeling philanthropic and rather pleased with myself, I pulled over and switched off. Here I was, tired and hot after a long day in the saddle and yet I was gracious enough to stop for this lowly shepherd and offer him water to cool his parched throat. I laboriously got off the bike, unstrapped my water bottle and offered it to him, a smug glow radiating about me like a halo.

He opened the bottle, smelled inside and cast upon me a look withering in its contempt: *"Vada!"* he ejaculated with curled lip, pointing to the river tumbling past just metres from his feet.

I got the feeling he was hoping for something a little stronger.

Chastened, I strapped my water bottle back on the bike, mounted up and rode on. (Offering bottled water to a Kyrgyz herder living in the wilds with a million litres of snow-melt tumbling past just metres from where he was standing must be one of the more crass things I've done in my life.)

So, in the stakes of "Let's see who can get into Tajikistan from Kyrgyzstan", it's Kyrgyzstan 2, Pommy bikers 0.

Just like the English football team in the World Cup.

It seemed like the "civilized" Silk Road I referred to the day before still had the ability to bite. It had twice blocked our way with an insouciant shrug, now forcing us on a detour thousands of kilometres out of our way.

A biker we had met somewhere along the road who had travelled through this area advised us never to take anything in the Pamir mountains for granted. He said he always applied for a five-week, multi-entry visa whenever he came to the 'Stans because you just never know when a road might be blocked by an avalanche or landslide, political or military unrest or whatever. Good advice. The highway itself had been closed for a few days by the army two weeks before we arrived because of some gunfire in the region; before that it had been closed because of violence between locals and Iranian refugees, evidently. With four continent-sized mountain ranges jostling and nudging and pushing against each other, all of them *still* rising as the Indian tectonic plate continues to crush itself into the Eurasian plate, earthquakes are a regular feature of this part of the world leading to avalanches and land slips which cover roads regularly. In fact, we became used to riding through sections of road that had clearly been covered by a landslide and bull dozed through, as well as passing battered graders and bull dozers parked on the side of the road near the most dangerous passes, ready for when needed.

A sobering fact: In 1911 an earthquake dislodged an entire mountain side into the Murgab valley, damming the river and forming a lake five hundred metres deep and sixty kilometres long, now called Lake Sarez. If the 770m high natural dam of rocks and mud were to fail, a disaster of Biblical proportions would occur, flooding deep into Uzbekistan, Turkmenistan and Afghanistan and wiping out everything in its path.

We came to realise that the thin strip of tar over this ancient and turbulent land gives nothing but a veneer of civilization; the teeth and bones of the land are still there beneath, just as they were when the Chinese merchants travelled this way.

I now realised just how right Kevin and Julia Sanders were when they wrote: *"It's an unpredictable road journey - extremes abound, whether it's the late winters and snowbound passes or natural disasters such as landslides and earthquakes. This is motorcycle adventure travel at its best. What more could you ask for?"*

Exciting times...

That night, over a meal, as were discussing the day's adventure and planning our next move, Gareth suddenly realised that it was his birthday.

Tajikistan

Girding our loins for the long detour, we headed off the next day with a feeling of resignation only to have Gareth very nearly taken out by a police car, blues on and siren blaring, followed by four 4X4s with darkened windows. Mafia controlling the police? Politicians? Sad if this is where the country is going; genuine, kind people being led by egomaniacs.

Actually, later in the trip we learned that, sadly, this is something politicians in Kyrgyzstan have now come to expect. This, I feel, is one of those indicator signs that a country is going to the dogs, that the rule of law, an independent judiciary, a free press are being hijacked by a corrupt political elite and the small people no longer have the power or courage to confront them and hold them to account. It's happening in South Africa. It's endemic in Russia, according to the Russian Black Bears motorcyclists that we met a few years ago. The most hated symbol of their leaders' impunity is the flashing blue light, or *migalka*, affixed to the top of officials' cars, which confers on the owner the right to drive on the wrong side of the road at high speed, ignore traffic lights, and careen onto sidewalks. It's got so bad in Russia now that if you are hit by a politician's car riding on the wrong side of the road or running a red light, it is *you* that are likely to be prosecuted. One of the Russian bikers mentioned a case which I've just looked up on the Internet and quote here from the Guardian:

"A railway worker has emerged as a national hero for Russian drivers after he was sentenced to four years in prison for causing a traffic accident that killed a regional governor.

Drivers across the country are calling for Oleg Shcherbinsky's release, in a sign of widespread disgust with government bureaucrats who terrorise the roads by driving at high speed in the centre lane.

Shcherbinsky was jailed after his car, which was turning off the main road into a side street, was struck at high speed from behind by the Mercedes of the governor of Altai region, Mikhail Yevdokimov.

Evidence given in court showed the governor's car was travelling at more than 90mph. Yevdokimov, his driver and a bodyguard were killed when the saloon flew off the road and hit a tree last August.

The judge ruled that Shcherbinsky was to blame for failing to give way to a special vehicle. He was convicted for negligent driving leading to death.

Motorists across the country have risen up in his support before an appeal hearing tomorrow."

These arrogant *Wabenzies* are the bane of ordinary, average Joes going about their lives in many Third World countries and emerging democracies, although the Merc has given way to high-powered 4X4s with tinted windows as the car of choice, driven at speed, pushing ordinary citizens into the gutters like rich men of old used to do on their horses.

Anyone who has tinted windows, I feel, is involved in something nefarious and ought to be arrested. It's a fact. If they're not doing something illegal then they're about to, so let's arrest them before they do. A pre-emptive arrest. I like the sound of that. If you're an honest, every-day bloke going about your business you don't need to hide behind tinted windows.

It's the same with dark glasses, trust me...

After leaving Kyzyl-Kyya fairly late in the morning because we had to check the bikes over carefully after our rough trip the day before, being rather naïve in trying to ride across a 3,300m pass on a goat track, the badly-maintained road made its way through congested streets in the rapidly increasing heat. With only a narrow corridor between the massive and almost uninhabitable Alau Mountain Range (highest peak 5621m) and the equally almost uninhabitable desert land to the north, it is understandable that most people will settle in the corridor between, especially as this contains Kyrgyzstan's main E-W road. But finally we left the dusty clutter of civilization behind us and started to make good progress towards the Tajik border.

Except that Gareth had made a rare navigation error. After a number of hours' travel along a hot, punishing road, we arrived unexpectedly at a border post and were told that, as we didn't have a visa for Uzbekistan, we couldn't proceed through the tiny speck of Uzbek territory that somehow got left behind in the middle of Kyrgyzstan. We had no option but to turn round and head back fifty kilometres along this execrable road to the missed turn-off pointed out to us by the soldiers on the goat pass. An unnecessary hundred kilometres we could have done without in the heat.

But the detour around the errant piece of foreign territory was a blessing: smooth as an infant's bum and almost new. We flew along at a blistering 65kph being awed by the incongruous spectacle that lay to our left and right: on the one side a desert so barren, hot and desolate it was frightening (not a sandy desert; one made up of what looked like eroded sandstone, hard and ungiving); on the other, a range of mountains so high that their heads played about in the clouds, snow-covered and stolidly formidible. In the middle, we rode along this good road encased in the oven of our riding gear, craving the wind-chill effect that did not come, just a dragon's breath of desert heat all over your body. The temperature was debilitating in its intensity. No wonder they seriously recommend one does *not* travel through the Karakum desert in mid summer.

This is a scary place.

Distances were far greater than we had imagined when planning the trip. In Central Asia, distances can't be calculated as one would in a normal country. It doesn't work like that. Shockingly bad roads - so potholed in places that it's less punishing for the bike to ride on the dirt verge - make travelling very slow. Nothing here happens in a hurry.

We finally reached the Tajikistan border; although we were the only people (other than an Iranian truck driver) at the border, it took one and a half hours to get through. Leaving Kyrgyzstan was a doddle. We dragged on our helmets and jackets yet again in the heat of the dusty border enclosure and made our way the few hundred metres to the Tajikistan border, got off the bikes, shrugged off jacket, gloves and helmet yet again and stood in the baking heat.

And waited...

Eventually we were waved through; the passport formalities were unproblematic. Back on the bikes to customs. Intense heat radiated back at us from the concrete and I could feel myself starting to burn. I poked my head into a cool prefab office and was looked at blankly by three faces. The men in uniform said nothing, just stared at me. No work was being done by any of them.

I gestured, holding up my passport and documents for the bike and smiling (always smile at border control officers - they might just hold your future in their hands) and pointed - *In? Out?*

Still without changing expression or speaking, one pointed a finger - *Out.*

I complied, closing the door and standing again in the oven of the dusty courtyard where we waited for another ten interminable minutes. Nothing happened. No one came in or out. No one entered or left Tajikistan.

Across the road was some shade under the verandah of a building so we went there discovering, to our delight, that it was a shop. And it sold cold drinks. We consumed these in the shade of the verandah while waiting another quarter of an hour before being summoned to the customs office.

An indication of the attitude to work of the three customs officials was that alongside the table with all the forms and stamps was a bed, enabling business to be conducted in a reclining, semi-reclining or sitting position, depending on your mood at the time. Opposite the desk was a TV tuned into a local station. Work - if one could call it that - would stop periodically while everyone paused to watch something on the telly. At one stage a news report was showing dead and bloodied bodies in the Ukraine.

Filling in the forms to allow the two of us and our bikes to enter Tajikistan took an hour.

The officials were friendly in a restrained manner, methodical and very very s-l-o-o-o-w.

But, finally, by 4.30 we entered Tajikistan. Third time lucky! At last we had penetrated its many and varied defences. There had been a number of times over the past few days when I thought it wasn't going to happen.

As evening approached, we found a cheap hotel (with working air conditioner). It wasn't long before we had divested ourselves of our heavy riding gear, showered and were sampling the local beer.

During the day and in the streets of Kanibadam where we stopped for the night, it was interesting observing how the locals (who are very different in appearance to the Kyrgyzs - more Iranian than Mongolian) cope with the heat: in public spaces the ground is constantly being wetted down with a hosepipe or water sprinkled from a tin, the water often taken from the many fast-flowing canals that criss-cross this land and even flow along the sides of streets; a bed placed under a tree, over a small stream, the water flowing between the legs of the bed; a restaurant where each table is surrounded by water in brick-built troughs and, just outside, sprinklers constantly spray water into the air - some of the strategies to cope with the intense, suffocating heat that makes life so difficult here.

Scary tunnel

The man wearing a uniform indicated we were to stop by pointing his finger to the side of the road next to a porta-cabin type building. Above their pockets was sewn the logo: "Innovative Road Care" - in English. Three more uniformed men clustered around us, asking the usual questions: *Where you going? Where you come from? How much does your bike cost?*

Then there were four or five. All wanted to shake our hands and welcome us - as has been the case throughout Tajikistan. We got out the map and they peered at it, pointing at place names they recognised, while others stared at the bikes and, particularly, the GPS. We showed them our intended route to the Pamir Highway and they made appreciative noises.

What their function was - *innovative road care* - that gave them the right to flag cars down, and just how this was "innovative" I have no idea but when, at last, they had finished their questions and we were ready to set off again, I heard one of them mention the word *chai*. It was about *chai* time and Gareth and I looked at each other and nodded.

In we all trouped, meeting a middle-aged man, also in uniform, stars on his epaulettes, who not only shook us by the hand in welcome but hugged us to the left and right (he stopped short of kissing us on both cheeks but I'm sure that was his intention).

Feeling like royalty, we were ushered into their common room and urged to sit on cushioned benches around a large table. Tea was duly made and bread produced; a watermelon appeared and was cut into slices. We were encouraged to eat. Throughout all this, a middle-aged woman sat in the corner of the room and diced carrots into a bowl then cut up bits of sheep - obviously preparing their meal. She glanced at us shyly every now and then and smiled, keeping out of the way but, when photos were proposed, she was there, posing with the rest of them. I handed round the photograph of my extended family, internet and postal addresses were exchanged and, after a most convivial half hour, we said our farewells and set off again.

Perhaps one of the reasons travel is so slow in this region!

We were flagged down quite often in the 'Stans: policemen, soldiers, guards - so typical of Third World countries and emerging democracies still clinging to the notion of the controlling state, the finger or baton indicating the exact position where one must stop to present the documents of your existence, explain why and where you are going, what your intentions are in the immediate future - demands that would be resented and resisted in a more mature democracy that sees the state as the *servant* of the people. But always, so far, the many interactions we had with authority figures were pleasant: a very positive greeting, usually shaking of the hand and questions that suggest interest rather than authority. Policemen have smiled and asked us to do a wheelie; soldiers have invited us to sit with them and share a meal - all most civilized and non-threatening.

The first two hundred-odd kilometres of travel since leaving that morning were most enjoyable, riding through low, fertile land on the edge of the mountain barrier, where mainly fruit trees are cultivated. Water melons and apricots by the bucket full were on offer under every shady tree on the side of the road; apricots could be seen drying in the sun, laid out on blankets; apricots littered the ground underneath the deep green leaves of the trees. Occasionally we came across women and children taking advantage of the heat by washing carpets on a convenient, flat surface - the road. Cars and trucks - and us - politely drove around them.

We continued steadily along a fairly good road for most of the morning although the fierce heat was a constant and unwelcome presence. Then, at last, we began climbing the first of two mountain ranges above three thousand metres that we needed to cross before reaching Dushanbe. Near the top of the first pass, we came upon the opening of a tunnel and were waved to a stop by a policeman.

As he walked towards us, I thought *Now what?* After pleasantries had been exchanged, he informed us sadly that we were not permitted to proceed through the tunnel. This in sign language, of course - hands gripping handlebars, right hand revving then arms held across his chest in a clearly negating X.

We asked why. I saw our attempt on the Palmir Highway receding once again: Kazakhzstan 3: Brits 0.

He pointed to some writing engraved in a plaque at the entrance to the tunnel: *Motorcycles and bicycles prohibited from entering this tunnel* he translated in sign language.

Gareth asked if there was a road around the tunnel, pointing at the surrounding mountains and describing a wide loop with his arm.

No, there was no way round.

He looked conciliatory and, using his hands, expressively indicated a motorcycle crash, then put his forefinger to his temple and pulled an imaginary trigger. Loose translation: "If I let you two jokers through this tunnel after I have been expressly forbidden to do so (and, look, it's even engraved on stone for all to see) and you are idiotic enough to have a crash, then I'm a dead man. I may as well just blow my own brains out because, if I don't, someone else surely will."

As you can see, I have developed a sophisticated understanding of sign language. Why, even before I left on this trip I could see that that stupid idiot, Thamasanqa Jantjie, signing in South Africa during Nelson Mandela's memorial service was talking gibberish. And being watched by the whole world - oh, the humiliation of it! Pity those in charge couldn't see it as well.

They should have asked me.

Anyway, we stood around, looking at inconsequential things for a while. It's best not to rush these things. After riding for days trying to get round the landslide, you don't just say, "OK" and go home when someone tells you that you're not allowed to go through a tunnel. Even if he's wearing a uniform. And we weren't even going to think of offering a bribe.

We waited.

He waited.

I got the water out and we had a drink. It was like sucking at the spout of a recently boiled kettle.

When enough time had elapsed for his dignity and authority to remain unblemished, he approached us and, in a low voice, (in case those who might put a gun to his head might be listening) muttered, "Just go quickly and no one will notice - you don't tell, I won't tell -" well, that's what his facial expression, conspiratorial tone and hand gestures implied.

We didn't need a second invitation; in seconds we had started our bikes and were heading for the entrance. It was a good tunnel - long and dark but perfectly serviceable - and both of us wondered why they had imposed a restriction.

But it was the *second* tunnel that was scary, though. And we realised - afterwards - that it was *this* tunnel we were being protected from, not the first. And only after we had ridden through it did we understand why.

Later, Gareth told me he remembered seeing on the map, somewhere around here, a warning in italics and with exclamation marks (well, I'm not so sure about the exclamation marks - but if there weren't any, there should have been) saying: "*Dangerous Tunnel!!!!!!!!!!!!*"

Well, *that* was an understatement!

We came around a corner near the top of the second mountain range and were confronted by a cluster of broken-down trucks, bits of gear box strewn in the dust, a few trucks haphazardly parked near the entrance to the tunnel; but from the black hole in the side of the mountain was pouring a thick pall of blue-black smoke. Gareth and I pulled over and switched off, both of us thinking the same thing: *a truck has caught fire inside*.

I am ashamed to admit - but this is an honest account and all my manifold weaknesses will be brutally exposed - that my first thought was not for the driver and his passengers being turned into toast inside that black hole and all the other drivers caught in there asphyxiating whilst frantically trying to reverse out; no, my first thought was: *Bummer, our way is blocked yet again...*

I didn't actually try to calculate how many days it would take for the tunnel to cool down and all the dead bodies and twisted, burned-out wrecks to be removed (which we did when trying to work out roughly how long it would take to bull-doze the rocks out of the cutting so we could get through), probably because at that moment two of the waiting trucks started up and began to move towards the smoking tunnel entrance. Both Gareth and I glanced quickly at each other and leapt on our bikes, starting them up and pulling in just behind the second truck: If they could get through, so could we.

The trucks crawled towards the entrance, both of us tucked in behind, so slow that we had to walk the bikes along to stop them falling over. We followed them inside, smoke billowing about us, the noise loud and oppressive. Then Gareth poked his head round the side of the truck immediately in front and pulled away; I followed, seeing just enough to hope that I wouldn't meet something coming the other way with its lights off. We made it past both trucks, our lights like two pale fingers probing the darkness in front of us.

As with any tunnel that is totally dark, it doesn't take long before you begin losing your sense of direction; with no points of reference, the mind begins to play tricks, you can no longer tell which is up or down; you have no idea where you are headed and your sense of balance leaves you. The easiest solution for me was to focus on the dim red point of light receding into the darkness in front of me that was Gareth's tail light and head for it.

I became aware - with not a little concern - that I was breathing almost nothing but exhaust fumes. The smoke wasn't smoke at all; it was diesel fumes. My throat felt raw, my lungs seared; my eyes began to burn. To add to the Stygian feeling of the place, the murky, swirling, stench of underground darkness, all about us was a noise so loud it threatened to overwhelm my senses. I tried to identify it, to place it, but couldn't. It was the kind of noise that makes your ears bleed; a noise that, in normal countries, you would be prosecuted for allowing your employees to work in; the kind of noise you might hear moments before a Kamatz truck rides over your head. And, in the darkness and smoke and chaos of the tunnel, it seemed, after a while, to be coming from the centre of my chest.

At first, the road surface was pot-holed tar. But this soon degenerated: most of the tar disappeared and the road - could it be called a *road?* - became broken and ridged. Everything was wet and all the potholes had filled with water. As the floor of the tunnel was also wet, the holes weren't visible - you just had to hit them and hope for the best.

We came upon more trucks trundling their slow way through and, taking a deep breath and praying that we wouldn't hit something or meet something coming the other way or be thrown under their wheels which thundered and bumped and splashed just a few inches from us, we overtook them.

Then, without any warning (because I couldn't see it) I fell into a deep, water-filled hole. The potholes and degenerated into craters that could cover half the "road"; and you didn't know what half because the entire floor of the tunnel - I keep on wanting to type "cave" because that's what it seemed like - was wet and running with water which glinted dimly in the headlights until suddenly *Whomp!* you'd go down again. Some of these lakes were hub-deep with sharp edges and, again, we had no option but to hit them and plough on, bashing and sloshing our way through.

Suddenly, the noise level increased (if that was possible); it felt like being on a runway with a 747 about to land on your head. I braced myself, not knowing what was about to hit me. Then out of the darkness appeared a *huge* industrial fan, the blades about ten feet high, with no protective grill. I was sure it was going to suck me in as I passed, spit me out again as a fine spray of blood and minced flesh. (Gareth said afterwards that he was worried a truck would kick a stone into the blades which would be shot out at us like a cannon ball. These fans were *sooo* big and *soooo* bad that a rock hitting a blade and being whipped out would punch a hole right through your helmet and head and bury itself in the engine block of a following truck.) And there was no warning; no lights; so reflective paint - nothing. Just out of the swirling, smoke-filled darkness and terrible noise appeared this monstrous *thing* and we only realised what it was once we were alongside it.

And, of course, all this time trucks were coming the other way, sloshing and bashing through the water-filled holes, some without lights or any reflective devices whatsoever. They just *appeared* in front of you, out of the gloom.

Suddenly, right in front of us, was a broken-down truck. Again, no lights, no warning, no nice man waving a flag. It was the first of three abandoned trucks we came across in the tunnel. (I don't know whether anyone ever checked whether there were dead people inside them, asphyxiated by the fumes. Probably not.)

Another thundering industrial fan to scrape past; more hub-deep, black holes to wade through.

Please, Lord, *don't* let me drop the bike in here!

That was my main worry (and my oft-repeated prayer). If I dropped the bike - and that was a definite possibility - no one would see me; Gareth would ride on, oblivious, until he came out the other side and realised I was no longer behind him. The trucks wouldn't see me before they had driven over me. Considering the condition of the "road", they probably wouldn't have even felt it. What's the *Bump! Bump!* of a motorbike or a body when you're driving underground through thick smoke across a murky bomb site in the dark?

A few more broken-down trucks and then, out of the gloom appeared an entire mechanical drill rig, just to one side but allowing enough space for one truck at a time to squeeze past, *working in the tunnel!* While trucks (and us) were bashing their way past in the darkness, this drill rig was digging out the ceiling! And there were workers in there, walking around like ghosts.

I wondered how many died inside there. I know I was getting worried that one of us might pass out. It took us at least fifteen minutes to get through the tunnel and we must have been inhaling, continually for this whole time, the amount of exhaust fumes your average suicide pumps into his car with a hose pipe to complete the job. I genuinely started to check my symptoms while I was riding and look closely at Gareth in front of me, wondering when one of us would fall over and die from asphyxiation.

But we didn't.

At last, through the gloom ahead, appeared a lighter patch which grew until, far ahead we could just make out the mouth of the tunnel. We were through.

The moment we emerged, both Gareth and I pulled over, switched off the bikes, dragged off our helmets, looked at each other and burst out laughing.

It was the kind of laughing you do when you've just scrambled into your 4X4 and slammed the door shut moments before the charging lion gets you; or when the car you've just rolled stops moving and you realise you're not dead.

Gareth, shaking his head in disbelief, exclaimed, "I think that's the worst thing I've *ever* done!" And for someone who's run with the bulls at Pamplona and done other stupid, dangerous things he hasn't told me about yet, that's saying something.

We both felt shaky for a while until our lungs had managed to clear the carbon monoxide and poisons and gunk our of our cells. We didn't want to ride on, wanted to pause and absorb the sheer ridiculousness of what we had just experienced; look back at the smoke and fumes pouring out of the tunnel mouth and think: *Have I really just done that?*

But I must admit another part of me rather enjoyed it. It's the sort of feeling you get just after saying to yourself, "This is a *joke* - right?" And there's nothing you can do about it so you just enjoy the moment, the *extremity* of it, because it's things like that that make memories in a way that watching hours of Judge Judy repeats or binge-drinking Friday nights just can't match (not that I'd know - I'm one of those strange men who've never experienced binge drinking on *any* night but, if given the choice, I'd take the Tunnel from Hell any day).

Only in an ex-Soviet country, a place like the 'Stans, would something like this be allowed. I mean, there were *workers* in there! I wonder, when they died - I say "when" advisedly because, in my humble opinion, no one could work and live in conditions like that for long - did they just send the body home and say to the wife and kids, "Sorry - industrial accident..." and hire another worker desperate for a job?

Travelling through this place sometimes gives me a feeling of trepidation that you just don't get when travelling in other places (well, not like Mogadishu or North Korea, obviously). And I'm not trying to be sensationalist here just to make the trip sound more daring, more adventurous. Throughout this account I have tried to express my thoughts and feelings exactly as they were at the time. Others would see it differently. And as we continued to ride the long, 420ks to Dushanbe, I was aware of this feeling deep down, aware of how tightly I was gripping the handlebars when riding down the passes, conscious of the oft-repeated thought: You could *die* out here, man!

It's not the people. They have been as open and welcoming as I've found in any country, if not better. In the very short time we have been travelling amongst the Kazakhs, Kyrgyzs and, now, the Tajiks, however fleeting and transient our contact has been, they have impressed both Gareth and me with their honesty, generosity and gentleness of spirit. We have been made to feel welcome in their countries, relaxed about our possessions and our persons; never once felt threatened or been worried that someone might steal something of ours left unattended.

No, not the people - it's the *country*. There is always danger in any extreme environment and this danger is compounded the more isolated you get. In the 'Stans, distances are vast, the terrain is either mountainous or desert with a few narrow bits in between - I generalise, of course, to make a point; and over the past two days we have experienced the shocking heat of the desert whilst, at the same time, being in sight of mountains so high that a human being, unprepared and exposed, would die up there. Today, as we rode into Dushanbe, capital of Tajikistan, the ambient temperature recorded on Gareth's bike while we were moving was 37C and, soon after we had stopped, it rose to 43. And yet, just forty minutes before, we had been riding across a pass with deep snow on either side of us.

If you are travelling through the mountains of Switzerland - probably just as high - you'd notice something of a difference; let's see: the road is so perfect and well constructed that you can relax while riding and enoy the biscuit-tin-lid view. And if you just happened to have an accident, an ambulance or helicopter will whisk you off to hospital in a jiffy while a breakdown company repatriates your bike.

Not here.

The road here is steep, the passes long, some of them going on for thirty kilometres or more. You never know, when coming round a sharp bend, whether you will meet a pothole in the middle of the road, unmarked (or sometimes with a line of rocks across as a warning, sometimes not), gravel, or a truck right across on your side because the switchbacks are so tight that many trucks cannot make them in one go. Most have to drive right onto the opposite side of the road, take the corner and hope they make it; if they don't, they then have to reverse and take another bite. So it's not uncommon, half way down, or up, a pass to come upon a truck completely across the road or even reversing at you in order to make the corner. Most drive with their bonnets up to get just that little bit more cooling into their engines in the intense heat. Sometimes you will come across a somnolent cow ruminating in its own little world of slow, bovine complacency, of masticatory ennui, in the middle of the road, or a flock of sheep that decide, on a whim, to dash across just as you approach like a bunch of lemmings causing you to take hasty avoiding action.

In Switzerland there will be a barrier, large and secure like a father's protecting arms, to prevent you from plunging to your death if you lose it on a corner. Not here. I think it was this, combined with the recollection, ever present in my mind, of my near miss on our abortive attempt to cross the goat-track pass, when I so nearly plunged off the road and into the river far below, that caused me to grip the handlebars until my knuckles turned white as I negotiated the passes. There are very few barriers here, just the road edge, nice and gravelly, and then a plunge thousands of metres down a rocky slope into the loess-yellow river at the bottom. On these unending switchbacks, it would be so easy to lose concentration for just a moment and you're on the gravel edge; and, once there, on a corner, you're going to go over. Where there was a barrier of sorts, this was made up of massive rectangular blocks of concrete, large gaps between, that looked more of a death trap than a safety net. Randomly placed, it seemed as if the road builders had made a decision to put up a concrete block every time a vehicle plunged over the edge using the logic: If someone went over here to their grisly death, obviously that's a place to put a large block of concrete with sharp edges so that, next time, when a truck (or motor cycle) sldes off on a bend, they've got two choices: miss the concrete block and get mangled tumbling down two thousand metres of mountainside into a river or hit the concrete block and break all the bones in your body on the sharp edges - it's your choice.

And the river! In Switzerland, snow-fed mountain streams are picturesque; people photograph them and put them on calendars. The water is clear and inviting, the kind of water that makes you think: I could go for a swim in here if it wasn't so cold. You imagine Swiss river water somehow smelling of sun-tan lotion washed from the bodies of the young and beautiful lounging about in brightly-coloured ski outfits, drinking cocktails and tanning their svelte bodies on the slopes.

Not *these* rivers. Here the water is not clear - it's a milky yellow, the eddies thick with froth from the mud of eroded mountain sides. As a kayaker, the holes and stoppers were the most scary I've ever seen. Rocks the size of trucks (maybe they *were* trucks that had not made some of the corners or whose brakes had failed down a pass) create holes so deep that, if you tried to kayak through them, they'd suck you down and hold you there in the mad, pulsing, turbulent darkness until, a week later, if you were lucky, your putrefying body would be spat out only to be sucked down again into the next hole. For forty to fifty kilometres or more (I wasn't checking; I didn't have time to look at the milometer in case I misjudged something and went over the edge) the road travelled above gnarly rapids whose grade, I'm sure, was off the scale. These were the kind of rapids experienced kayakers, on a drunken night out, would decide to run just to see how many of them could come out alive at the bottom. Continuous violent rapids, vast elephantine pulsings of water alongside the road, sometimes close by so you could smell the death in it, sometimes so far down that it was a mere thread making its way between steep-sided mountain slopes, but always waiting to kill you if you were stupid enough to go off the road.

And the mountains; vast enough to bend the earth's crust by the sheer weight of them, so high you have to crane your neck to see their peaks. But it wasn't so much the high, rocky, snow-capped ones that were frightening. Somehow, the white snow is comforting, pure and clean and... well, Swiss. It's the desert mountain ranges that induce a feeling of trepidation, immense bulks of rock and sandstone, scree the colour of dead things collecting in vast slopes at their bases, the heat that radiates off them, devoid of life.

I realise that I have indulged in a certain amount of hyperbole here. I've done so on purpose - not in a self-indulgent spirit but in an attempt to explain my feeling of deep-down fear travelling through this place, a feeling that was, of course, balanced by the sheer wonder of the land through which we travelled, its vast, stark, isolated beauty - but a fear that was very real and often there: *A person could die out here. A person could really die out here...*

Six long days to get round the landslide at Sary-Tash. Of course, at that time, and for the next week, we were never sure whether the Taldyk Pass had been bull-dozed open or whether we might have to retrace our steps along the whole of that road to get back again.

International hotel = fancy breakfast, right?

Having finally arrived in Dushanbe, we had to book into a "quality" hotel to get our passports validated. Only expensive hotels do this, and I wouldn't even know where to start to get it done myself - much easier just to present it to the receptionist and say, "Validation?" and they do it for you.

So we booked in to some fancy international hotel recommended by Lonely Planet - can't remember the name but maybe I should have so I could tell everyone who reads this and might be thinking of visiting Dushanbe: *Whatever you do, don't stay there!*

On our bike journeys we try, as far as possible, to eat local and sleep in cheap rest houses/hostels/home-stays whenever we can. This is mainly to cut down on costs but also, in that way, you get closer to understanding how the ordinary people of a country live. Although, to be honest, after a long day's riding when we arrived in a town dripping sweat and ready to drop, we usually took the first room in any establishment offering hospitality, regardless of condition or cost. The thought of turning down some room because it was too expensive or egregiously bad and heading off into the heat and the traffic to find another more suiting our pockets or taste was anathema when exhausted on the side of a street in 43 degree heat, with the prospect of a cold shower and a colder beer just minutes away. No, we just took whatever was on offer with a sense of profound relief - with some interesting experiences, as a consequence, along the way.

Deciding to rub shoulders with the *hoi polloi* is great - you will eat local food, mix with local people, get a feel for the sounds and smells that characterise a place and give it its distinctive ambience. But, when choosing to do this, you must be prepared to eat what is put in front of you, sleep where someone indicates, defecate in whatever hole is on offer. And in poor countries this is often not what you would necessarily choose for yourself. How we yearned, over the weeks in the 'Stans, for a toilet we could sit down on, a toilet that at least offered you the choice of using paper to wipe your bum (often there wasn't even *water* provided, so I have no idea what the locals do) and that wasn't swarming with flies and stinking so badly that you worry you might pass out and *die* in there. Often there is a metal grate over the hole - understandably; the image of a child falling through is unthinkable - but this usually just catches... well, I'm sure you get my drift here.

Where food is concerned, eating local in poor countries usually means consuming what is readily and cheaply available, usually anything that's running about outside and can be caught and killed. No flights from across the world bringing chilled lettuce and strawberries all year round. Throughout the world there are always chickens scratching about in the dust somewhere and usually grain of some kind so the universal breakfast tends to be "omelette" - two eggs broken into a pan and sloshed about - dry bread and black tea. Milk is almost unobtainable because there are seldom fridges or electricity. *Sour* milk, yes. Suppers are usually whatever two or four-footed animal or bird is readily available to have its throat slit, starch of some kind and black tea.

Here, in Central Asia, it's usually *Shashlik* (bits of sheep with bones on a skewer) and dry bread; in Ethiopia, it's cold foam rubber with small piles of piquant salads (actually *injera* - disgusting stuff; fermented teff made into foam rubber you could use to replace your car seats); in sub-Saharan Africa is usually road-kill and rice.

I exaggerate.

A bit.

So, if you've gone local and you've eaten goat's eye-balls and intestine stew and you've only paid $5.00 for your room, plastic slip-slops and stinking squat toilet thrown in, you've got nothing to complain about. Lots of colour to regale your friends with when you get home.

But the point I'm trying to make in this rather long-winded and circumlocutious way, is that our "International Hotel" here in Dushanbe (well, they charge in US dollars so I assume they have that pretension) was as crummy as only an ex-Soviet hotel can be. We had our stolidly-built, mono-browed *babushka* guarding each floor, making sure we didn't misbehave, steal the towels or, heaven forbid, bring someone off the streets with the intention of doing something naughty; an air conditioner that sounded like a vintage tractor starting up; towels and toilet paper (at least they provided some - maybe that's what makes it an International Hotel) that would work well as an exfoliant. But, we felt it was worth paying the $80 just to get our passports registered with the Powers that Be so that we didn't get arrested and have our fingernails pulled out.

Until, that is, we found out that, in enlightened Tajikistan, unlike its North Korean clone brothers, Uzbekistan and Turkmenistan, you no longer have to have your passports registered within a few days of entering the country. It seems they have entered the twenty-first century at last. Only, the ebay-bought Lonely Planet guide I was too parsimonious to buy new, now seven years out of date, had stipulated that, on pain of death or lengthy incarceration, it *had* to be done.

Ah, well, we thought, at least we'll have a good breakfast for our $80. International Hotel = fancy breakfast, right?

So, the next morning, bleary-eyed and sleepless because of the noise from the air conditioner, Gareth and I made our way to the breakfast room, a spring in our step and expectation on our faces, anticipating ice cold yoghurt and freshly-squeezed orange juice with condensation beading on the rim, a selection of cereals with cold, full-cream milk, strong cups of good quality coffee, perhaps sausage, eggs, bacon... well, you know what I mean.

After weeks of dry flat-bread, black tea and "omelette", we were salivating for it, especially, strangely enough, for cereal and cold milk.

We found the room. It was bare, except for some tables covered with plastic cloths and cheap plastic chairs. In one corner was another table holding an urn and two containers with tea bags. We sat down, hoping there had been some mistake; that, any minute now, smiling waitresses would flounce in with laden trays and smiles.

The solitary waiter who did emerge a short while later was dull-eyed, sullen and male. His impassive face was sunken and pock-marked. Gareth whispered that maybe he was a recoveree from one of the Soviet germ warfare testing stations on Vozrozhdeniya Island.

He didn't even attempt to communicate, just dumped in front of us two plates of noodles with a spoon full of greasy meat on top. No coffee; selection of...

We picked at the glutinous mess, feeling cheated and more than a little annoyed. Next came a fried egg and piece of red sausage. You had no choice - no: *How would you like your eggs this morning, Sir?*

And black tea.

Gareth asked for some milk.

Our diseased waiter answered monosyllabically, "No milk."

Gareth insisted.

"No milk," the pock-marked, sullen one insisted.

Gareth got up, entered the holy sanctum of the kitchen with a purposeful step and asked the Boss-Man inside for milk. A short while later, two glasses of warm milk arrived.

We so wanted to find a manager and say, "Please, do yourself a favour: send just one of your senior managers to *any* humble B&B *anywhere* in the Western world for just one night and learn how things ought to be done."

And when we checked out we *so* hoped the lady at reception would ask (with a sweet, engaging smile), "Did you enjoy your stay?" so we could give vent to our frustration - but it wasn't to be. Phrases like *Did you enjoy your stay?* (or sweet, engaging smiles) are not really on the menu in most of these places. When we approached with our key, the grim-faced, gold-toothed lady behind the front desk continued working on some piece of paper for five minutes before gracing us with her unsmiling attention.

In the end we said nothing. It wasn't worth it.

So, the point I have been laboriously making is this: When you pay peanuts and go local, you take what's put in front of you and you like it. But - *dammit!* - when an establishment charges you inflated prices in dollars and poses as an "International Hotel", then you expect a certain degree of quality.

And when you don't get it, it makes you cross.

Another army check-point

It was a ball-breaker of a road, the track from Dushanbe to the bottom of the Khaburabot Pass; a bike-breaker of a road. A road with few redeemable features to grace its sorry life. If it were a dog, you'd take it out into the back garden and shoot it as an act of kindness in case it was rabid and bit someone.

When we set off that morning I vainly hoped we might make a marathon 525k push to Khorog where, in my mind's eye, the Pamir Highway really begins. But, despite leaving at eight thirty and reaching Kalaikhum on the south side of the Khaburabot Pass by just after six, totally exhausted, we had only made it half way.

The Pamir Highway (although some dispute this) actually begins further west in Afghanistan then travels through Dushanbe, Khorog, Murgab then north to Osh. As there are very few viable ways to cross the high Pamir Mountains, this trail had been in use for millennia as little more than a trading route for camel trains and formed one link of the ancient Silk Road. Soviet engineers turned it into a road capable of carrying vehicles in the early 1930s to ensure the swift transportation of troops and equipment during their stand-off with the British over Afghanistan. Off-limits to travellers until recently, the road has been allowed to deteriorate through over-use by heavy trucks and poor maintenance. There is tar in places but mostly it is bad dirt.

At the end of the day I knew that. Every muscle in my body knew that.

The first fifty kilometres were great - cool morning air, good tar road, 60kph - and I stupidly thought to myself that it just *might* stay like that all the way to Khorog. And we'd be there, fresh and ready to tackle the notorious Pamir Highway the next day.

But we were already *on* the Pamir Highway and I could see why it's often preceded by the adjective "notorious".

The good road became poor; the poor road bad; the bad soon became execrable. We were struggling to maintain 40kph, hammering the bikes unmercifully. Both Gareth and I said to each other at some point during the day, as we had done before and would do many times afterwards, that we wondered just how much punishment a motorcycle can take before bits of it start to fall off, to give up and die. How a mono-shock is able to take the constant punishment of absorbing the weight of a loaded bike over back-breaking tracks hour after hour, day after day is beyond understanding. Why the bikes didn't just fall apart I can't explain.

When a tar road goes bad, it's a terrible thing. When it first becomes distressed, it begins to crack. This is no problem; you ride over the cracks and hardly notice them. Then potholes appear. Again, this is not much of a problem because, if you are vigilant, you just ride around them. But it's when the potholes become so big that more of the road is pothole than tar that a road becomes confused and dangerous. It doesn't know what it is any more. It loses its identity and turns feral. Because the bits of tar that remain, dark patchy islands in a narrow sea of dirt, have sharp edges, usually about four to six inches high, which can bend a rim, burst a tyre or your shock absorbers if you hit them at speed.

For at least 180ks on that day we rode over a feral track, unpredictable, mailgn, devious. And we just had to ride over it - there was no choice (other than packing up and going home) -

grit your teeth and aim for the bits that looked least lethal. Riding a bike along a road like that all day is like beating a puppy and listening to it cry. It's impossible to look around and enjoy the scenery because if you take your eyes off the horrible, rutted, potholed track for more than a moment you'll hit a cricket-ball sized rock, fall down a massive pothole, ride into a somnolent donkey who finds the heat of the road pleasantly soporific, slide on gravel or ride off the side of a cliff face and die.

There's little pleasure in that kind of riding, punishing a bike for hours and wondering just how long before something breaks.

I realise that, over the last few paragraphs, I have been almost unconsciously anthropmophising the road. I suppose when you are travelling along a road or track that engages the whole of your attention all day, it takes on a personality of its own; becomes a friend or an enemy; works with you or fights against you, trying to hurt - unlike the anodyne impersonality of a motorway.

During the day we noticed that my left pannier couldn't take it any more and had split in half. I lost my heavy bike lock but, fortunately, the rest of my gear was being held in by the last few threads that were still intact. Gareth's panniers, too, were taking strain and beginning to fall apart (maybe there's wisdom after all in using the expensive aluminium ones!)

At about eleven Gareth nearly lost it on a corner and realised he had a puncture.

"Why is it always me?" he wailed as I checked the score. Unlike England's soccer team, I am 4-0 up on the puncture stakes. Gareth's KTM seems to attract sharp objects.

I like to tell him it's because he rides badly.

Now, did I mention that it was hot? I think I have once or twice before. We were on the side of this baking dirt road, no shade anywhere, facing the prospect of forty-five minutes grovelling in the dust to repair the puncture.

Not relishing the prospect, Gareth asked me to ride ahead a bit to see if there was any shade, which I did.

At the bottom of the pass I could see a few buildings and a tree so I rode back; we pumped up the tyre and set off quickly to see if we could reach the shade before the tyre went flat again.

We parked the bikes under the tree. A few metres away two men worked on the gearbox of their van. Under the shade was a truck selling watermelons. My mouth began to water.

Gareth got out his tools and crouched alongside the bike. Without being asked, a Tajik man, small and wiry, black trousers, black vest and sandals, embroidered *zarina* on his head, hair and beard cut short, crouched next to him and began to help. I quickly realised that I was redundant so topped up our water bottles and bought a watermelon, trying to cut it up with the small blade on my utility knife. The men from the truck saw me struggling and brought over a carving knife which they meticulously wiped clean before offering it to me. I cut the melon into slices, consumed a few and offered the rest to Gareth, the Tajik man and some children who had gathered around to watch.

Having no English at all, this man just quietly worked with Gareth, squatting in the dusty shade under the tree, as if it was a perfectly natural thing to do. I suppose for him it was. They found a four-inch nail sticking through the tyre and pulled it out. The tube had ripped, a hole larger than any of the patches we carried, and Gareth was about to throw the tube away and replace it with his spare when the Tajik man shook his head, picked it up and, beckoning us to follow, carried it to one of the small, square buildings, about the size of a single-car garage. There, incongruously, in the middle of nowhere, just happened to be a roadside tyre repair workshop. We stood back while they repaired the tear with a large, oval patch, replaced the tyre on the rim and pumped it up. After they had re-fitted the wheel - again,

I found myself pleasantly redundant so ate some more watermelon - we asked if we could pay something for the repair. The Tajik man wouldn't take anything for himself but asked that we pay the owner of the tyre repair shop an amount that, when converted, came to $1.00.

It is this kind of serendipity, this selfless assistance from ordinary folk that one brushes against as one passes through their countries, that makes a journey less of just covering distance from town to town and more of a life experience.

Shortly after this, we stopped at a road-side shed to top up our fuel and experienced the first of many re-fuellings from a bucket. This was always done in a most professional way, the petrol taken from a large drum stored in some dusty garage, transferred to a metal bucket crudely marked to measure litres and squashed at one edge to form a spout. Fuel was never spilled or wasted and, unlike our plastic bottle refuelling in Africa, no one attempted to rip us off.

After we set off again, I glanced at my GPS and noticed it was suggesting that, in 360 metres, I needed to turn right. Thinking that a little odd, I glanced at it again a minute or so later and it was still requesting a right turn after 360 metres. And then I realised it was 360 *kilometres*. So, basically, judging by the average speed we were managing on this road, we would need - according to my GPS - to hang a right at about - what? - lunch time tomorrow. (Actually, it turned out to be four pm.) Another indication that, through these mountains, there just are no alternative routes; that if an avalanche or landslide covers a road there are few ways round that will not take long days of effort.

We battled on until mid-afternoon when we came across a Russian biker, loaded for travelling. We stopped to chat and share information on the route. He informed us sadly that the road ahead was closed.

Our hearts sank.

We questioned him further: About ten kilometres ahead was an army control point and they would not let him through. The road was closed. He had even tried to bribe the soldiers but they hadn't taken the bait.

So, that was it. Strike four. Tajikistan had won.

Looking at the map, there were only a few roads around the stoppage; all would require us to back-track all the way to Dushanbe. Most headed somewhere up into the mountains and stopped there, going no further. Dead-end tracks. But there was one road that headed south from Dushanbe to Kulyab and then east to join the Pamir Highway again that might give us a route around. However, taking that route would involve a three hundred kilometre stretch of now notorious dotted-line track along the Afghanistan border to Kalaikhum - and, after our previous goat-track experience, we didn't relish that; and, anyway, if the area had been closed down by the army, what was the likelihood that *all* other roads into that area would not similarly be closed?

We bid our disappointed Russian biker adieu and pressed on, reaching the army control gate shortly thereafter. Unaccountably, however, the soldier on duty studied our passports and visas, filled out all the forms and waved us through. Perhaps our Russian friend had been denied access because he was *Russian* - the Tajiks getting back at their old masters for their crimes and atrocities over the past decades of Soviet control and domination.

Who knows and who were we to ask questions? Relieved, we quickly made our way past the raised barrier before the soldier changed his mind and headed up the Khaburabot Pass, following a delightful, *honest* dirt road, a joy of a road, technical enough to keep you focussed but not a bike breaker. It's roads like these, high and wild and remotely beautiful, that make a trip like this worthwhile and compensate for the long sections of bad dirt.

Finally, by late afternoon, we reached Kalaikhum and found a pleasant home-stay right next to the river which roared past, full of snow-melt, at the speed of an express train. Such a feature was it that our resourceful home-stay proprietor, limping with a deformed left leg, had built a platform out over the water with a low table and some chairs so one could relax and eat just metres away from the frenetic roar of the water.

At last we were within touching distance of the town where, in our planning, I felt our real adventure would begin - Khorog - where the Pamir Highway turns west and you have the choice of continuing on the highway or turning further south and taking the smaller, more remote road that follows the Afghan border and the Whakan Corridor.

This protruding finger of land has an interesting history: designed many years ago during the period known as The Game, when Russia's expansion to the south through the Palmir Mountains met Britain's expansion north through Pakistan, Afghanistan and the Hundu Kush. Two of the most powerful nations of earth eyed each other belligerently and squared up to one another and spied on each other, each trying to seek an advantage. Finally, accepting the stalemate, the Whakan Corridor was built into the map as a buffer zone between the two competing super powers.

And here, I felt, our journey would really begin...

An historical digression

As you probably know as little about the 'Stans as I did before my brief skim through Lonely Planet (and most of what you *do* know comes from watching *Borat: Cultural Learnings of America for Make Benefit Glorious Nation of Kazakhstan)*, here are a few historical snippets about these ancient cultures, shoved into a corner by the bicycle sheds and discarded fag butts of the world between Russia, China, Pakistan and Afghanistan; countries of yurts and goats, the Silk Road, Genghis Khan, the dying Aral Sea and Samarkand. (That's about all I knew of the 'Stans other than the haunting photograph that Gareth sent me - of high and empty mountain slopes and remote dirt roads edging their way into a pale sunset that was the conception of this trip.)

(NOTE: Pretty much all of the following has been unrepentantly lifted from Lonely Planet, most copied verbatim, sometimes artfully paraphrased by me. Some of the small words like "and" and "the" and the occasional deep, insightful comment are mine.)

Long ago, as the great civilizations of the East and West developed separately and independently, what little contact between the two was made possible by the Silk Road, a fragile network of shifting intercontinental caravan tracks that threaded through some of Asia's highest mountains and bleakest deserts. At any given time any portion of the network might be beset by war, robbers or natural disaster: the northern routes were plagued by nomadic horsemen and a lack of settlements to provide fresh supplies and mounts; the south by fearsome deserts and frozen mountain passes. The road had its origin in China, dividing after leaving China through the Jade Gate; the one branch skirted the dreaded Taklaman Desert while the other headed south, meeting again in Kashgar before heading up a series of passes into and over the Palmir and Tian Shan mountain ranges. Once over the mountains, the road split again, one branch ending in Iran, the Levant and Constantinople, the other leading to Mesopotamia and north Africa. Trade flowed both ways but, perhaps more important, so did ideas, and the Silk Road became, in a way, the world's first information superhighway.

Here in the heart of the largest landmass on earth, vast steppes provided the one natural resource, grass, required to build one of this planet's most formidable and successful forms of statehood: the nomadic empire. Grass-fed horses by the millions and mounted archers remained the unstoppable acme of open-ground warfare for more than 2500 years.

Alexander the Great arrived in about 328BC and he and his troops did some raping and pillaging (his troops are still being blamed for the occasional blond-haired, blue-eyed Tajik - yeah, right!); various tribes fought and dominated each other and the Chinese, who tried with limited success to wall them out for the next few hundred years. Then Genghis Khan with his 200,000 soldiers swept across the central Asian plains doing more raping and pillaging, burning cities and trampling Islamic holy books underfoot in the city streets. Genghis himself ascended the pulpit in the chief mosque in Bukhara declaring, "I am God's punishment for your sins," before burning the city to the ground. They then continued their slaughter, plundering Samarkand, Kabul and most of Eurasia.

(An interesting aside: Dr Julia Pongratz of the Carnegie Institute of Global Ecology claims that Genghis Khan's murderous conquests "killed so many people - estimated at over 40 million

- that huge swathes of cultivated land returned to forest thereby removing nearly 700 million tons of carbon from the atmosphere. And, although his methods may be difficult for environmentalists to accept, ecologists believe it may be the first ever case of successful man-made global cooling.")

So, Genghis Khan was the founder of the world's first ever Green Party. Slogan: "For every person you kill, you save 17.5 trees!" (I did the maths.)

Might catch on. Don't let Kim Jong-un or Mr Putin find out.

Back to the 'Stans:

Civilization in Central Asia took over 600 years to recover from Genghis Khan's depredations. Just as life seemed to be settling down again, they were colonised by the Russians, who proceeded to rape and pillage in a different but nonetheless similarly heartless way.

(Well, it's a lot more complicated and convoluted than that but I'm assuming that if you wanted to know about the detailed history of the 'Stans you'd be reading a history book and not a motorcycle travelogue.)

The Russians had built a line of fortified outposts on the northern fringe of the Kazakh steppe and trade developed. Still mostly nomadic and pastoral, Russia's neighbours to the south seemed anachronistic and unstable, ready for assimilation. With new currents of imperialism sweeping Europe, the Russians looked around and realised that the nearly empty lands on their south western border had potential as vast as their equally vast landscape, with a mostly nomadic population ripe for the taking. The British were expanding inland from India into Afghanistan and the Russians needed a secure southern border.

The first to fall were the Kazakhs. Exhausted and traumatised by so much bloodshed and inter-tribal rivalry, the Kazakhs gradually accepted Russian "protection" during the mid-eighteenth century, but St Petersburg interpreted that to mean permission to annex - so they did, sending "excess to requirement" Tartars and Cossacks to settle and farm the land.

(Are we witnessing a re-enactment of this rather successful Russian policy in the Crimea and Ukraine now, I wonder?)

Understandably, the Kazakhs weren't particularly chuffed about this and revolted. In response, the Russians stripped the ruling khans (the last rulers directly descended, by blood and throne, from Genghis) of all power and formally colonised their land, dealing a crushing defeat on the Tekke, the largest and fiercest of the Turkmen clans where their last stronghold, Geok-Tepe, was captured with up to 16,000 Tekke killed. With the last resistance crushed, the Russians pressed on until they reached the Afghan border in 1885 and there they paused.

In a mere twenty years, the Russians had extended their territory by an area half the size of the USA, an ethnically diverse, economically rich swathe of land that they proceeded to exploit with joyful abandon over the next century, using the 'Stans as a seemingly inexhaustible human, mineral and agricultural resource.

(As much as I love Russia and the Russians, they do have a penchant for treating people like cattle, and the countryside - especially other people's countryside - like an expendable resource. Or as a dumping ground for nuclear and biological waste as well as any people whom they feel are being annoying.)

For the next few decades Britain and Russia proceeded to eye each other suspiciously over the Pamir Mountains and the Hindu Kush.

The American Civil War ended Russia's imports of American cotton so she began to look towards her new Central Asian colonies to fill the gap. Railway lines were built; enterprising Russians saw potential in these new lands and over a million settled in Kazakhstan alone. The local pastoralists became alarmed at this invasion and resentment grew. The Uzbeks rebelled in 1897 but, like the Kazakhs, were brutally put down.

Then came the First World War. Millions of Russian soldiers on the front line needed food and massive herds of Kazakh and Kyrgyz cattle were requisitioned for the war effort; other colonies were forced to provide cotton and food. As the war limped on, and Russia bled men, the tsar needed more to fill the gaps in the line.

Millions more.

In this war, as in the next, Russia sacrificed men with reckless abandon, losing approximately 9,150,000 men (76% of all mobilised forces). In WW2 it was worse - 22-28,000,000 soldiers and civilians were killed defending the Motherland, 13.7% of their entire population. In both natural resources and human flesh, the Russians seem to regard all as necessary sacrifices to the common good, the concept, particularly during Communism, that the maintenance of the state is more important than the rights (or life) of the individual, that mankind must be subservient to the state at all costs. And when you put low value on individual life, you will lose a lot of people.

On orders from the tsar, local people in the colonies were conscripted as non-combatants in labour battalions. Significant to these resentful people was that their men were "requisitioned" not "mobilised" - a term usually used for cattle and materiel. Human beings were being treated as the property of the State to do with as it pleased, a living resource to be tapped at will.

Understandably, the Central Asians said no. It wasn't their war. Uprisings began and swept eastwards throughout 1916. Reprisals were harsh. Men were massacred, villages burned, women and children carried off. Russian troops gave up all pretence of being a 'civilizing influence' as whole Kyrgyz and Kazakh villages were brutally slaughtered or set to flight. Manhunts for suspected perpetrators continued all winter, long after an estimated 200,000 Kyrgyz and Kazakh families had fled towards China. The refugees who didn't starve or freeze to death on the way were shown little mercy in China.

Then came the Russian Revolution in 1917 and the tsar was toppled. The Central Asian Russian colonies began preparing for freedom and self-rule. It was a short-lived hope. The first attempt at self government in Kokand was quickly smashed by the Bolsheviks with more than five thousand Kokandis massacred. Peaceful co-existence was obviously not an option favoured by the fledgling Communist state.

From the start, the Bolsheviks were hated by the locals who resented their overbearingly dominant presence. Worse even than the tsar's bleed-the-colonies-for-the-war policies, the Bolsheviks levied grievous requisitions of food, livestock, cotton, land and forced farm labour. Trade and agricultural output in the once-thriving colonies plummeted. The ensuing famines claimed over a million lives.

The new Communist policy of forced collectivisation attempted to catapult a once-proud nomadic, pastoral people from their centuries-old feudal lifestyle into that of communism and a settled agrarian culture that would produce food for the Motherland. The intention of the First Five-Year Plan (1928-1932) was to eliminate private property and, in the case of the wandering Kazakhs and Kyrgyz, to put an end to their nomadic lifestyle.

The response of these proud people was simply to slaughter their herds and eat what they could rather than give them up, leading to famine which lasted many years. Resisters were executed and imprisoned. Millions died. Stalin, it seems, deliberately used meagre food resources to induce famine in an attempt to control and subjugate the people's will and to depopulate Kazakhstan, making way for Russian expansion.

But after the fall of the tsar, many people began working towards national liberation and democracy, forming - usually clandestinely - parties, movements and factions. But by the late 1920s Stalin had had enough. These benighted individuals on the periphery of the vast sprawl of land that constitutes Russia were becoming a thorn in his flesh, especially the intelligentsia. Throughout the 1930s Stalin "eliminated" all dissenters. Thus began the systematic murder, called the Purges, of untold tens of thousands of Central Asians. Arrests were usually made late at night. Confined prisoners were rarely tried. Mass executions and burials were common. Sometimes entire sitting governments were eliminated this way.

Starting in about 1924, Russia drew lines on the map and arbitrarily created the states of Kazakhstan, Kyrgyzstan, Tajikistan, Turkmenistan and Uzbekistan. Before the Russian revolution, the peoples of Central Asia had no concept of firm national borders. The soviets, however, believed that such a populace was fertile soil for Pan-Islamism which they regarded as a threat. Each new Stan was given its own ethnic profile, language and history. Where an existing language or history was not apparent or was not suitably distinct from others, these were supplied and disseminated. (Seems like George Orwell got it about right.) Each of the new republics was shaped to contain numerous pockets of different nationalities, each with long-standing claims to the land. Thus divide-and-rule laid the groundwork for weak and disputatious nations who would be controllable by a powerful central Russian government and never gain enough internal unity to become a threat.

WW2 led to further changes to the Central Asian 'Stans. As Hitler rather foolishly invaded Russia in a fit of hubris, whole factories were dismantled, loaded onto trains and sent to the relative safety of the 'Stans where they were re-assembled and continued producing for the war effort. These factories remained after the war, boosting their 'Stans' meagre economies.

But, as is so common in Russia, other things forcibly moved to the outer reaches of the USSR were people. Koreans, Volga Germans, Chechens - in fact anyone thought by Stalin to be a threat to the state was deported. These new citizens put down roots and now form sizable communities in all the former Soviet Central Asian Republics.

It is said by some that, such was the hatred of their Soviet masters, that over half of the 1.5 million Central Asians mobilised during WW2 deserted, many of them joining the Germans against their hated Soviet masters.

Other effects of Soviet control of the republics, treating them as tethered milk cows, was the policy of "encouraging" each republic to specialise in a limited range of products, which made their individual economies dependent on the Soviet whole. In Tajikistan the world's fourth-largest aluminium plant was built - but all the aluminium ore had to be brought in from outside the region, keeping them dependent and vulnerable. The Uzbek republic was developed to supply most of the Soviet's cotton, making it the world's second largest cotton producer after the USA. To supply the masses of water needed to grow the cotton, they diverted the waters of two rivers, the Syr-Darya and the Amu-Darya, while downstream the Aral Sea was left to dry up. (What's a mere sea when you're dumping millions of people there?)

Then, in 1954, Nikita Khrushchev launched the Virgin Lands scheme, using the vast steppes of Kazakhstan to produce wheat. Massive (everything the Russians seem to do is *massive*), futuristic irrigation schemes were drawn up to supply water to the formally arid grasslands, with water taken from as far away as the Ob River in Siberia. Large numbers of Russians were resettled to work the farms. The initial gains in productivity soon dwindled as the fragile exposed soil of the Steppes literally blew away in the wind.

The resettled Russians, however, remained.

Then, in 1979, the Russians invaded Afghanistan in a vain attempt to prop up the crumbling communist regime on their doorstep.

Bad move. They forgot to read the history books. No one wins a war in Afghanistan. After ten years which cost the lives of some 15,000 Russian soldiers (and 1.5 million Afghans), the Soviets called it a day and pulled out. It seems they (and others before and after them) finally met with a nation of people even more stoical than themselves, who were and are prepared to make impossible sacrifices of human flesh to maintain their independence, shedding lives and blood until they wear out their invaders by a calculated process of attrition.

And so, near the end of the century, the Soviet system collapsed. By 1991 all of the five republics had declared their sovereignty.

But none was prepared for the harsh reality of independence.

The fall of the Soviet Union sent the Central Asian republics into an economic collapse. Suddenly, a system that had been designed to be held together by the economic power of the mighty Russian state lost its centre and things fell apart. It is has been estimated that the depression that followed was three times greater than the Great Depression of 1930s America. The republics, now independent, were home to 16% of the USSR's population and 64% of its poor. Kazakhstan found itself with nuclear weapons and a space programme.

Now, the iron-fisted regimes of Uzbekistan and Turkmenistan have completed their slide into pariah states, where political abductions, torture and trumped-up charges are commonplace and where stagnation is regularly confused with stability. Drug smuggling is a particular regional problem and the soaring rise in domestic drug use is fuelling some of the world's fastest growing rates of HIV/Aids, especially in Kazakhstan, where infections are doubling annually. Central Asia now has an estimated half a million drug users.

The end of the old Soviet subsidies meant a decline in pretty much everything. The deepest economic trauma was in the countryside but even in the cities many professionals earn under $100 a month. But the most heart-rending are the old, especially the Slavs, whose pensions were made worthless overnight with the devaluation of the rouble. Throughout the 1990s, one of the most common sights across Central Asia was watery-eyed *babushkas* sitting quietly on street corners, surrounded by a few worthless possessions for sale, trying not to look like beggars.

Suddenly the Soviet era began to look attractive again...

So, you've now had a brief potted history of the 'Stans. Thanks Lonely Planet for doing all the hard work and for not giving me a hard time for lifting, plagiarising, summarising and personalising the closely-packed, twenty pages of detailed history of the Central Asian republics in your Central Asia guide. Much appreciated.

Of travel and travellers

Both Gareth and I nearly died today.

Well, I exaggerate a little for effect, but death could very well have been the end result for both of us.

Gareth first: We had been stopped at yet another army checkpoint, got off the bikes, stripped off our gear in the heat, collected our documents. We were asked to enter an almost bare room, furnished with nothing but a desk against one wall. From the ceiling, a bare bulb hung from a drooping flex. As we made our way across the room towards the desk, one of the soldiers grabbed Gareth and dragged him back. He had been about to walk into the electric wire from which the light was hanging and which had been casually joined by twisting the bare wires together. Because most Tajiks are somewhat vertically challenged compared to us Westerners, the bare-wire join was a few inches above their heads and, therefore, by Tajik standards, as safe as houses. But for Gareth, being tall, the wires were level with his forehead and he was within inches of walking into them. And I seriously doubt that there was anything as sophisticated as a circuit breaker in that bare room.

Now my near-death experience: We had stopped for a rest and a nibble in a local eatery just off the road. Sitting at a low table (which we shared with an extended Tajik family), we imbibed watery soup with lumps of gristle removed from, I assume, the leg of an ancient sheep. I had a massive piece of this gristle in my mouth and was attempting to dispose of it with some degree of dignity. Because I am a reasonably polite person, I didn't want to spit it out so, after a lengthy stint of vigorous mastication and making no headway on the knee joint of this aged beast, I decided to swallow it whole.

It stuck in my throat.

Now, again, trying to be polite and not make disgusting regurgitating noises, I thought I'd give it another try.

It wedged itself even more implacably in my gullet.

I then discovered, somewhat to my surprise, that when one has a fist-sized piece of gristle stuck on one's throat, one can't breathe. It was a rather disturbing discovery. Maintaining an outwardly calm demeanour, I attracted Gareth's attention by prodding him and, being one of the sharper knives in the drawer, he immediately asked, "Are you choking?"

I nodded and turned my back to him, expecting the Heimlich but, instead, he beat me in the middle of the back three times, each time harder than the last.

"Is it out?" he asked as my vision tunnelled. I saw a cone of bright light inside of which I'm sure I could see winged creatures beckoning to me in an encouraging and enthusiastic manner.

I shook my head and he hit me again, harder still - and the lump of gristle emerged, much to my relief.

It's a disturbing experience, nearly dying, and one I wouldn't like to repeat. I don't recommend it. What if Gareth had been fiddling about with the bikes outside or visiting the toilet, locked away behind a metal door somewhere at the back of the place? Not a pleasant thought.

I asked him why he didn't Heimlich me straight away and he said he was about to if his last blow hadn't worked. But he probably relished the chance of legitimately beating his Old Man and paying me back for past inadequacies.

Riding on after lunch, I occupied my mind - strange things go through my head during the solitude of long bike rides - by thinking of our joint funeral back home. Someone would come up to my wife and say in hushed and respectful tones, "Well, my dear, at least they both died doing what made them most happy. Tell me, was it skidding off the road on a high, wind-swept pass and drowning in the turbulent water of the Pyandzh River? No? Was it being kidnapped by the Taliban and shot because they refused to renounce their faith? Was it dying of hunger in the remote wastes of the Wakhan Corridor after being trapped for a week by avalanches? Oh... Did your husband die of a heart attack when propositioned by a tanned, lithe-limbed young lady-cyclist who found him irresistibly attractive?"

And my wife would answer dryly, "No such luck: Gareth walked into a low-slung, live electric wire and my idiot husband choked himself to death on a piece of gristle."

Where's the dignity in that?

It was a long, hot ride to Khorog where I assumed the *real* Pamir Highway would begin. Of course, we'd been riding the highway ever since we left Dushanbe and, other than the delightful Khaburabot Pass, it had been a disappointment. Before the trip, in my mind, I was expecting something more remote, more extreme; I was anticipating terrain that demanded a certain degree of technical riding ability.

But the road, so far, had required more endurance than skill; a test of just how much sustained punishment and heat bike and rider could take.

We'd met a number of travellers on the road but, interestingly, more bicyclists than motorcyclists, most of them doing marathon overland trips - all respect to them. And German and New Zealand tourists, mostly middle-aged, with their guides "doing" the Palmirs. It rather takes the cachet out of our journey, becoming somewhat old hat.

But, during the day, we met a number of interesting and unusual travellers who, as they always do, widened our understanding of and respect for the human race.

First, along the road, we met an experienced German biker and stopped for a chat - as you do. Speaking fluent English with a pronounced American accent, he told us that he'd been travelling through the Palmirs on his own for a while and, in the process, had gleaned some information about do-able tracks in this area, tracks that we had identified in the planning stage before we set off and which we had marked on the map with a, "Yes, I'd like to do that!" comment, in particular the road that follows the Whakan Corridor along the Afghan border and leading to the very remote point where Afghanistan, China and Tajikistan meet. And, if we could get our timings right, there's a market just across the border into Afghanistan - you cross the river on a footbridge - and, evidently, travellers are allowed across into Afghanistan on each Sunday morning without a visa.

This biker had our respect. He was travelling alone, his BMW X-Trail 650 well kitted out - lean and mean, no frills, nothing for show. He was using soft luggage which was well secured, spare fuel container bolted onto the bike in a custom-made frame. He'd travelled around the Palmir Mountains last year, left his bike in Bishkek for the winter and returned this year to ride again. Because he knew the area well, we got out our map and asked him to point out some of the lesser used roads and passes we might like to attempt. He did more than this, showing us where fuel could be obtained, how to escape the attention of some of the army checkpoints, and so on. He'd just ridden the Bartang Pass - alone - but warned us of high water on the river crossings. Evidently a Belgian biker recently lost his GPS on the pass and couldn't find the track again after a long river crossing.

This pass, the Bartang, ("...rarely accessed... many landslides...") is regarded as one of the high points of adventure travel in this area and a route we had marked as a "must do" - but, having had to ride all the way round to get onto the Pamir Highway because of the landslide, whether we could do it or not was now uncertain.

He mentioned, also, that there had been some shooting in this region a week or so before and all permits to cross were being denied. Interesting: he, too, dismissed the Pamir Highway as somewhat *passé* (again, not his word, but that's what he was implying) and spoke with a curled lip about bikers on big GS's whingeing about the Wakhan Corridor road being too hard, too sandy. (He didn't mention large, expensive aluminium panniers but I know he was thinking it!)

After a pleasant and informative chat, we bade each other goodbye and rode on.

That night, ensconced in a very comfortable home-stay (with sit-down toilet, *nogal!*), we met a German couple travelling in a well-equipped, heavily-used Land Cruiser, seasoned travellers who had explored most of Africa and were now concentrating on Central Asia. They were looking for a workshop that would weld their exhaust that had broken off at the manifold on the bad roads. We needed to buy a pump. I had discovered when unpacking that I had left my partially destroyed pannier at our last home-stay, in one of the pockets of which was our electric pump. There's one thing you really cannot afford to travel without in a very remote region and that's a tyre pump. It would be extremely foolish to attempt it so we would have to look for one before we set off the following day.

Then there were the two British bikers who were heading for Afghanistan but the Irish guy had his XR400 stolen within a few days of entering the country; wanting to continue with the trip, he'd bought a local Chinese cheapie, all chrome and plastic, that everyone in this area rides.

A Swiss couple into their fourteenth month of travelling by bicycle from Switzerland, across Europe, Turkey, Iran and on into Central Asia were staying at the home-stay as well and it was good talking to them about their travels. Both Gareth and I have nothing but admiration for these cyclists who bear the heat, the bad roads and the high passes using just their muscles to keep moving. *No engine!* Re-*spect!*

While chatting earlier in the day to the German biker with the American accent, I asked him what nationality he was and he replied, "There's no need of nationalities -" and he's right. When you're on the road and you meet fellow travellers of like mind, nationality becomes of little consequence. Fortunately, almost without exception, all the travellers we have met speak good English.

That night we all - Gareth and me, the two Germans and the two Swiss cyclists and a cat - shared our meal together outside as the sun sank below the mountains and the air cooled, sitting cross-legged on rugs around a low table in the Arab style, reminiscing and sharing anecdotes about our travels. Sipping my beer, I relaxed into a mood of Bohemian decadence and, while we talked, I understood more profoundly the young German's comment: *There's no need for nationalities.*

Someone mentioned two guys who have just become the first people ever to walk across the Bearing Strait from America to Russia (in mid-winter, obviously, while it was frozen, but they did carry flotation devices to get across any open leads).

(Come to think of it, *not* the first people to cross the Bearing Strait; we assume our Neanderthal ancestors did it long ago - but that was during an ice age so I suppose it doesn't count.)

And the Russians arrested them! (Not the Neanderthals, of course - the two guys.) Way to go, Ruskies! In almost every other part of the world, if you pulled off a stunt like that, you'd be front page news; they'd drive you through the capital city on an open-topped bus and grant you the freedom of the city. There'd be bunting and cheering crowds. But the Russians arrested them and threw them in prison because they didn't have a permit or they'd strayed into a "forbidden zone". Or maybe they did have a permit but it lacked the correct stamp. Russians - don't you love 'em!

The Swiss cyclists are doing something truly epic: fourteen months, eleven thousand miles so far and, they told us with relaxed smiles and a wonderful sense of comradeship, "We will keep going as long as it's fun and the money lasts."

Gareth and I have decided that any couple contemplating a long-term relationship ought to be required to do a challenging trip by bicycle, motorcycle or 4X4, camping - preferably in the extreme heat or cold - before they finally make their decision to cohabit. Our logic is this: If you can stay together under these conditions you've basically proved that you will stay together no matter what is thrown at you; also, it's only when put under stress like this that you truly get to know someone, understand what they are really like, how they will react when good turns to bad and nice to ugly.

I think they should make it a law.

At nine thirty that night a French-born American and his young Russian wife arrived at the home-stay on their bicycles. These two had cycled down from Russia and are going wherever... however...

They told us how their tent had blown away on one of the high passes while they were packing up and they couldn't find it again. They are looking for another before they ride on.

Thinking about the trips these cyclists are making makes me wonder why I am writing this; what is its function?

I suppose if we were kidnapped or shot or something really dramatic happened it would make more worthwhile reading. I question my narcissism in writing this account of a fairly mediocre trip when compared with our cyclists and those men who walked across the Bearing Strait...

Every biker in the world

We left Khrog quite late the next morning after a most civilized, languorous breakfast shared with our travelling friends, reclining on soft rugs and cushions at the low table outside under a tree, before the sun rose high enough to heat the air. We then headed for the bazaars in town to try to buy a pump. After an hour or so, communicating by dint of a piece of paper torn from my notebook on which Gareth had drawn a crude representation of a hand pump attached to a flat tyre, we managed to track one down - a cheap, plastic, Chinese bicycle pump that could have been supplied as an accessory with Barbie Ken on a bicycle. It was rather ambitiously labelled "BEST PUMP" - a case of devious mis-selling or some Chinese manufacturer not fully aware of the quality of opposition products. But it was all we could get and Gareth assured me it would suffice to get us out of a jam, although he was pretty sure it wouldn't be able to pump up a tyre sufficiently to seat it on the rim. (In this he was wrong, though, because, pink plastic toy that it was, it did the job and pumped both his front and rear tyres, after three more punctures, hard enough to enable us to continue our journey all the way into Kazakhstan.)

Then it was a quick 110ks to Ishkashim along a fairly good dirt road where we would turn east until forced north again by the Chinese border.

For much of the day we followed the path of the Pamir River, slow and wide and benign, unlike the raging, turgid rivers that had been our maleficent companions over the past five days; Afghanistan was just a stone's throw away across the water, the desert-like slopes of the Hindu Kush Mountains rising from the valley to dominate the sky on our right, the dry peaks snow-capped and remotely beautiful; and on our left, the Shakhdara Range, with Karl Marx peak (6723m) and Engles Peak (6507m) somewhere just to the north of us, testimony to the Soviet connection with this area. As we rode, the air cooled because of the altitude and the proximity of the river just a few metres below the level of the road, and I was able to relax and enjoy myself, no longer having to worry about plunging to my death from a height of thousands of feet.

At long last we were travelling through a terrain I had expected the Pamir Highway to resemble and I remembered with a pang of joy that was strangely like pain, when, six months ago, Gareth and I had looked together at this very track on Google Maps, using the satellite photograph facility to trace the road we were at that moment riding along next to the Afghan border, imagining the possibility of us, one day, *being here*, realising it was unlikely, a dream rather than a certainty.

And now we are here.

The image from Google Maps, transferred into my brain, had materialised into a dirt track which I could *feel*, every bump and curve, its patches of soft sand beneath my wheels, seeing the river clear and blue, gently moving between boulders just to our right.

At last I felt we had achieved what we had set out to do; at last I was able to say to myself: *This is what we came here for!*

Strangely enough, we had achieved this *not* riding the Pamir Highway, which we found a disappointment, clogged with Chinese trucks and worn to a state of bike-breaking disrepair.

But alongside the Wakhan Corridor! Ah, now, *there's* a road to soothe a world-weary biker's heart, a track that knits up the ravel'd sleeve of care!

And, while riding during the day, I thought to myself, if I could just take this road and its surrounding mountains, put them in a box and transport them to some place more accessible, I would make myself a fortune; I would be a very wealthy man. Every biker in the world would want to ride it - again and again. A *joy* of a road!

At some point we had to fill up; we managed to find petrol in a road-side shed, the fuel transferred to the bikes by hand in a milk churn, and then we began to climb towards the high Alpine plateau of the Pamir Mountains.

We continued riding alongside the Afghan border until, as evening approached and the Alpine desert landscape around us began to soften, we reached the small town of Langar. Partially hidden amongst the rocks and dust and low, scrubby trees, we found a quaintly ramshackle home-stay run by a man who could have been Kenyan and who spoke passable English.

The air was cool at last at 2800m, yet, despite that height, the surrounding mountains made us feel small and insignificant with their their far-off peaks perpetually snow-capped against a pale sky. A cold wind blew sand about the courtyard where we had parked the bikes, smudging the distant mountains with dust haze.

We unloaded, dumped our stuff in a large room with brightly-covered mattresses on the floor, and sought out the shower. In a squat, rectangular building across the stony courtyard I found a bare room containing a rust-stained bath. Managing to work out how the cranky taps worked, I washed while sitting on a plank over the bath, a car rear-view mirror screwed into a piece of wood for shaving.

Later, driven inside by the wind and dust, we reclined on the usual raised platform, covered with brightly-coloured rugs and pillows, and drank cheap local beer sold in one-litre plastic bottles from tea cups decorated with blue flowers. Sharing a beer with us was Marco, a garrulous Spanish cyclist who had, to Gareth's great jealousy, just "done" the Bartang Pass.

A short while later we were joined by the rather lovely Italian-Australian Georgana, making her way alone by public transport through the 'Stans after having spent some time in Iran, who proceeded to excoriate Marco for drinking the last cold beer, her abuse softened by a coquettish smile...

Also there were an insular Dutch couple in a well-appointed Land Cruiser on their way to Malasia. This couple - whether because of their Seventh-Day Adventism or through personal choice - kept themselves to themselves, cooking, eating and sleeping in their 4X4. They had incurred the disdain of Georgana earlier in the day by not stopping to give her a lift. Considering that she had been standing on the side of the road in the dust and heat and bustle of some nondescript village for six hours that morning, dying for a pee and not being able to find anywhere discrete when they drove past, it is understandable why she didn't feel particularly chummy towards them. But she was philosophical and didn't bear a grudge. (Unlike towards poor Marco, who had committed the unforgivable sin of drinking the last cold beer).

Personally, I find it difficult to understand the Dutch travellers' insularity and their leaving her stranded - surely offering to help a fellow traveller is part of the experience of the road and, having a stranger sharing your vehicle for a period of time must be an enriching experience. You get very few obnoxious travellers and, if someone is *that* objectionable, you can always ask them to get out of the car. And mixing with fellow travellers in the evening, sharing a meal and good conversation, surely, must be one of the high points of any journey. But they chose to stay huddled in their 4X4, absorbed in their own company.

Anyway, Georgana was generous in mentioning in an off-hand manner how they had left her stranded and didn't vilify them as she might have done - just treated it as a strange quirk of humanity. Poor Marco, though, the Catalan, the one who drank the last cold beer, came in for the light-hearted lash of her coquettish tongue.

"*Selfish bas***rd!*" she berated him while he laughed, enjoying her attention as only a man can savour the vilification of a beautiful woman.

Oh, how she lashed him, repeatedly reminding him of his ungentlemanly behaviour and mocking his Catalan pronunciation.

"Say 'The man lay on the beach' -" Georgana cajoled with wicked intent. "Say it... go on, *say* it -"

"The man lay on the bitch," Marco obediently intoned to our peals of laughter.

"Say 'Please change the sheet,'" she insisted, lounging with us on brightly-coloured cushions at the low table. "Go on, *say it!* Inviting me to have a beer and then drinking the last cold one, you macho *bas***d!*"

And Marco repeated obligingly, "Please change the s**t!" humouring her, accepting her tongue-lashing as if it were praise.

Her mocking abuse, evidently, was not occasioned by his consumption of the last cold beer alone. What had happened was this: In desperation, after standing in the heat on the side of the road for six hours, being ignored by the Dutch couple who left her there and drove off in their fancy 4X4, not being able to get a lift, she haggled with a local taxi driver who eventually agreed to drive her to Ishkashim (the other drivers were asking extortionate prices, trying to take advantage of a woman travelling on her own, no doubt). But as soon as she had got into the taxi, along came Marco on his bicycle only to be persuaded by her already drunk taxi driver to indulge in a little further consuming of alcoholic beverages while she waited impatiently in the car.

"Macho bas***d!" she exclaimed, hitting him playfully on the arm, a punishment he accepted with good-natured stoicism.

She seemed completely at home, communicating with our Kenyan-looking host in the local dialect ("*I picked up some Farsi while travelling in Iran*" - as you do), legs tucked under her loose skirt, bare arms making a gesture in the pale yellow light of a candle as there was no electricity.

Our conversation that night as we reclined around the low table eating our meal together - Georgana-led, now that I come to think about it - focused on gender issues and the complexity of relationships. She related how, when travelling alone, she is more hassled by local women than the men - although they (the men) give her a hard time as well. How the women would touch her, even feel her breasts as if fascinated by European flesh, constantly asking why she wasn't married, why she didn't have children - a tedious, cultural thing, she admitted. We spoke about how procreation differs from a man's and a woman's perspective; about women's reproductive clock, always there in the background, always running down; society's expectations. We discussed marriage and vegetarianism, of Marco's calorie intake to enable him to cycle the vast distances he did every day, something that gave him considerable pride. Georgana told us about groping men - how some men will take the opportunity provided by an injured woman on the side of the road - or, as in the case of my sister, immobilized by a stroke in a hospital bed in Cairo - to grope them under cover of a show of giving assistance; about women cyclists trying to take a pee and being photographed by bus-loads of Arab men and, for a moment, I felt ashamed of my gender...

And so the evening waned with the flickering of the candle and we gradually fell silent then drifted off to bed: Gareth and I with the next stage of our journey to negotiate, Marco facing another 50ks of dirt road on his bicycle and Georgana hoping to persuade the Dutch couple over breakfast to give her a lift to the next town.

Second day alongside the Wakhan Corridor

Throughout the day we met only one other vehicle - a local man driving his ancient truck taking two cows somewhere further up into the mountains. Later we came across a pair of Korean adventure cyclists, a young man and his achingly pretty girlfriend and we stopped briefly for a chat, poring over the map together discussing road conditions and such-like. Before we headed off again, leaving them and their bicycles in the loneliness of this vast landscape, we gave them some water as their bottle had developed a leak.

Later during the day we came upon yet another barrier across the road where it turns north and re-joins the Pamir Highway. Our plan was to continue east towards the Chinese border going past Lake Zorkul, a restricted area for which you need permission to enter. We had managed to secure this permission a few days earlier in Khorog.

We stopped at the barrier, together with the driver of the old Russian truck and chatted while we waited for the first soldier to appear. There is obviously so little traffic on this road that to man the barrier probably seems absurd so the soldier on duty goes home and waits there until he hears a vehicle approach.

Eventually a soldier appeared and, after checking our papers, raised the barrier and let us through, not realising we would be taking the track that continued to follow the Afgan border towards China. But, not being able to find the correct track, Gareth and I were doing some cross-country riding, looking for a break in the fence or a gate. As soon as the soldier saw what we were doing, he shouted after us and told us to wait while he fetched his superior officer.

We switched off and waited. Eventually the officer came, and speaking no English at all, only Russian, informed us that we could not proceed. It was forbidden. The road was closed.

We were able to understand that there had been hassles in the past with travellers straying into Afghan territory and, as a consequence, problems with Afghan soldiers. Because of this he could not let us go. If we caused conflict with Afghanistan then not only would he be in trouble but he would have to sort it out.

Not wanting to give up, having come so far, we persevered. We showed him our map and our intended route, pointed out the GPS and demonstrated how it would prevent us from straying over the border. We showed him our slips of paper, "Special permission to enter Zorkul Region", rubbing our fingers together to show that it had cost us money. We must have been sufficiently persuasive because, after a long, thoughtful pause, looking carefully at our map and the GPS, he stood back and pointed towards the barrier.

The soldier lifted it for us and we were through.

From there we began a slow climb to above 4000m, the land opening up into a wide Alpine valley, the Hindu Kush peaks not so high above us any more, but still a few thousand metres higher than the high mountain plateau we were riding across. The gravel road was in good condition enabling us to maintain a steady pace for the next eighty kilometres, mostly standing on the pegs, looking out across the Alpine desert landscape with the ever-present mountains in the background and I found myself saying aloud in an ecstasy of fulfilment, "We're here! We made it! We're here!"

Separating us from Afghanstan was a crystal-clear, slow-flowing river, the cold water gathering from snow melt higher up the valley, a warm sun overhead. At mid-day we took a break and rested on its bank, above us the sky indigo blue and busy with clouds, six camels and their herd boy just across the river, Afghanistan so close that if there had been a soldier there, we would have been able to speak to him in a conversational tone; Gareth, sleeves rolled up, threw rocks into the river while I attempted to capture the scene in my note-book, the tinkle of water all about us loud above the silence of the mountains.

By late afternoon the road had become narrower; a short while later it degenerated further into two wheel ruts worn by the tyres of passing vehicles. And when a track becomes little more than wheel depressions winding their way across a landscape, you know you are pretty close to the goat track, the faint dotted line on the map.

Finally, on the upland plateau at 4300m the wheel ruts themselves became vague and meandering and, for a while, we lost them and had to cast about the rocky terrain a bit before we found them again, relying on the GPS to keep us headed in the right direction.

This was the kind of remote landscape I had been looking forward to when we planned the trip. And, at last, we had found it.

Somewhere in the middle of nowhere I saw a rude stone- and mud-built dwelling off to one side of the road, small and square with a flat roof, built low as if bracing itself against the cold. A young child stood alone outside, watching as we rode past and I decided we should stop. I so wanted to meet some of the hardy Tajik people who scrape an existence from these high, cold desert plains and this seemed too good an opportunity to miss.

Gareth, riding in front of me, hadn't noticed them and carried on but I was confident he would, at some point, realise I wasn't behind him and turn back, which he did about ten minutes later. For a while I was a little concerned, though, because the track was pretty faint and I felt there was a chance we might lose each other completely.

In moments there were five ragged children, including a baby in arms, mother and grandmother clustered about my bike, probably wondering where on earth we had descended from. The grandmother invited us in for *chai* and we accepted gladly.

We entered their rude dwelling, the clay floor and walls bare, rocks showing through where the mud plaster had fallen out, a rough, home-made wooden door to keep the wind out; inside, a low, raised rock ledge had been built for sitting and sleeping on and, to one side of the door, was a crudely made metal stove, the wall blackened behind it, the chimney passing through the roof. On the stove, a battered kettle and a pot.

That was all. There were no toys, no decorations, nothing on the walls or floor to add comfort to their sparse living conditions. The old lady, rake thin and wearing a blue dress, could have been Mother Theresa - she had that same sweet smile, that gentleness of spirit so often lacking in people you meet in the Western world. Missing many teeth, her skin leathery and brown, she had an inner beauty that drew one to her as she quietly prepared tea, smiling encouragement to the children who watched us shyly. Her daughter, too, was thin, less strikingly beautiful, more retiring; her face, like her mother's, was worn by the sun and the wind and the cold, etched with the strain of living in these demanding conditions. Both women wore head scarves, as did the two older girls, one of whom could have sat for Vermeer's *Girl with a Pearl Earring;* although still a child, her skin was already burned a dark brown by the harshness of the elements. She was beautiful.

The children had on a mixture of clothes, worn through on elbows and knees, their hair matted and unkempt. The Vermeer girl wore a jerkin hand made from sheep skin, the wool turned inwards for warmth.

I took the youngest child, a dirty-faced infant of about two, on my lap where she sat contentedly while tea was being made. The two women fussed over us, making sure we were comfortable; then they brought bread, two bowls of sour milk, a bowl of thick cream with something else in it, a bowl of butter and two spoons. They watched us while we ate, touched by their generosity in the midst of their obvious poverty. In our panniers, we had some emergency rations left so we unpacked these and gave it to them so they wouldn't go without.

Having no shared language at all, I offered them a photograph of our family, which delighted them. Gareth gave the children some pens and brightly coloured post-it notes to play with. I wanted to ask where the men-folk were but couldn't make myself understood in sign language. There were no animals about the house but, clearly, they were pastoralists, probably keeping a herd of sheep from which they were able to sustain themselves with milk and meat. I can only assume the men were out somewhere in the mountains looking after their flocks.

Sad to leave them and moved by their welcome and their generosity, we finally bid them farewell and continued on our way, the sky clouding over and threatening rain.

As the afternoon waned, Gareth suggested we stop and camp for the night so we rode on until we came across a small lake about five hundred metres off the track and set up our tents. Dark mountains silhouetted close behind us, the high peaks of the Hindu Kush in front beyond the small lake, there was a sense of isolation, of silence and solitude one could almost touch. With the setting of the sun, the air turned very cold and it started to snow. Using the last of the light, Gareth worked on his bike, trying to sort out the power and fuel problems but without success.

We had given away all of our food to the Tajik family earlier in the day - except for some powdered milk and muesli, but that would be more than enough for our supper and breakfast. Driven inside by the cold and snow that had begun to fall, we ate our muesli supper in my tent and then retired for the night, wearing all our clothes against the bitter coldness that comes with such altitude.

It is difficult to understand how anyone can live in this place through the winter.

As I lay in my tent listening to the silence, aware of the remoteness of our camp and our isolation, I came to the conclusion that I had achieved all I set out to do on this journey. If we were to see or experience nothing further of note, I would deem the trip to have been a success. Before that, I have to admit, I was disappointed - days of bike-breaking, corrugated, rocky and truck-congested roads, bathed in sweat, covered in dust. There had been very few moments of transcending joy that one would expect on a journey like this, moments that would become absorbed in one's mind and memory to keep and treasure into the future. I wanted more.

But after the pain came joy. The battering we had experienced over the past ten days only made the delayed pleasure of travelling through this wildly remote landscape all the more worthwhile.

Finally, I had experienced over the last two days the best motorcycle riding in my long life and, as for travelling in *any* vehicle, second only to the experience of driving across part of the Western Sahara in my little Ford Fiesta as part of the Plymouth-Dakar Old Bangers Rally.

A truly amazing two days' riding.

As far as I'm concerned, you can have the Pamir Highway; give me instead the remoteness of this route alongside the Wakhan Corridor, its stark beauty and isolation, the sparseness of its population, its unpredictable weather, the gentle, winding track...

That evening, in my tent, I reflected on the day...

Riding has been brilliant - 105 miles of biker heaven, 30-40mph on the pegs almost all the time, berms and whoops making it feel like a fair-ground ride but with just enough of the nasty stuff to keep you honest - sudden dips in the track where a river has cut a wicked gouge across; occasional deeply-buried rocks protruding high enough above the road surface to rip your sump out if you are careless enough to hit them; river crossings, dry and wet, full of round boulders; deep holes, large enough to bury your front wheel, that some furry little buggers the size of a badger dig in the road; stretches of soft sand that can catch you unawares, sensing the front wheel find its own way. Fortunately, where the very big holes are concerned, holes that, if you hit them, would swallow your front wheel and break your neck in an instant, are usually marked by local drivers who place large rocks in the road to give you fair warning (so long as you don't hit the rocks, that is).

My bike purred like a pig in muck all day, thinking to itself (just like I was, a human/machine empathy): I've found my raison d'etre, my soul, my zen; I am in bike Nirvana; I am living what my Oriental designers had in mind when they created me; I have fulfilled my potential in life and am, at last, supremely happy.

Gareth's KTM, on the other hand, is struggling with the altitude, drinking fuel at an alarming rate and losing so much power at low revs that he continually has to ride the clutch when bumping slowly through boulder-strewn river crossings or climbing steep ridges of rough gravel that we need to cross or nasty tight bits in the road, just to keep the bike going. Evidently a sensor has failed and it can't work out how high it is and, therefore, how much fuel to pump into the engine so it probably thinks, Ah, what the Hell, I'll just err on the generous side.

This is what happens when bikes become too intelligent and start getting beyond themselves...

The pedestrian bridge

We are ensconced in a pleasant local "lodge" in Murghab, the highest town in Tajikistan at 3630m. It is clean, the rooms bare of all but carpets and a mattress on the floor, wash in a bucket of icy cold water but a welcome touch of comfort after a hard day's riding.

The day could be split into two halves: the fantastic and the gosh awful.

I'll start with the fantastic.

We woke after a cold but comfortable night to the sound of rain but, as the sun rose, the clouds disappeared and we emerged from our tents to a bracing cold day (in fact, it snowed on us a few times during the morning), bundles of cumulus clouds white against the deep blue of the sky and, all about, the snow-covered mountains of the Wakhan Range on our left and the Southern Alichur Range rising above us on our right.

With Gareth's bike using so much fuel we had to choose our route carefully. The plan was to fill up at Jarty Gumbez but, when we finally got there, the "town" consisted of about four houses and a precarious footbridge across the Istyk River. It seemed deserted so we walked around looking for someone to ask about petrol but the only thing moving was the river, ominously deep on the far side. Eventually someone appeared and we asked for fuel; the man pointed to a small cluster of buildings across the river.

"How do we cross?" we asked using sign language.

He indicated with his fingers that we should walk across the footbridge.

We unstrapped our three Rotax containers from the bikes and carried them across the bridge. The buildings were deserted. After nosing about for a while, we managed to find a man who said that there was fuel - he pointed to three twenty-litre plastic containers stacked next to a broken-down van - but we had to wait for his boss who was coming at about 1.30.

Three hours to wait. We placed our empty fuel containers next to his full ones and repeatedly tried to get him to change his mind. Eventually, we managed to understand that he was telling us his boss would "F*** him up if he sold petrol to us" so we didn't press him further.

Now low on fuel, we had to take the direct route to Shaimak then north to Murgab, and this required crossing the river. The alternative was a long detour north then east to Cheshtebe (or Cheshekty, depending on which map you look at) then back to the road to Shaimak. This would take us too far out of our way - we would never make it on the fuel we had left - and there were no other "towns" (read: *cluster of 4-5 houses*) along the way.

We looked again at the river. Could we cross it? Although wide and shallow in places, on the inside of each meander the water was deep and blue and running hard, too deep to see the bottom; there was no way we were going to get the bikes across. In addition to that, the far side bank was very steep, rising almost straight out of the water and covered with loose stones and mud - impossible to climb with the loaded bikes.

We asked the man again how we could get across. Again, he pointed at the rickety pedestrian bridge.

"The *bikes?"* we asked, pointing, unsure of whether he had understood.

He nodded and smiled encouragingly.

I didn't believe him. The bridge was too narrow, too lightly constructed to take the weight of the bikes.

We walked over to inspect it. Made by welding two truck chassis together, it was covered with wooden planks of dubious strength. Where planks had rotted through, patches made from flattened tins had been nailed onto the wood to cover the holes. To provide a semblance of stability (safety?), a cable had been strung across at just above knee height on the right hand side and various bits of wire strung from this to the truck chassis to hold it in place. The left side was bare except for a 10" pipe supported on logs. It was so narrow I was convinced we wouldn't get the bikes across, especially as, at the far end, the bridge met a wooden building and one had to make a very tight, right-angled turn to get past.

Gareth's comment was, "Take my bike across; if we get it through, then we know yours will."

We unloaded everything, carried it across and piled it on the other side of the river. Then Gareth tentatively rode his bike onto the bridge. It was so narrow that his legs wouldn't fit next to the bike when he came across a metal stanchion or a log holding up the pipe. With some careful manoeuvring, me pulling on the front wheel and Gareth climbing over obstacles while trying to ride the big KTM, we managed to get it across and round the turn on the other side. Gareth was through. I followed a few moments later.

This was a relief. The road was now open as far as Shaimak and we had sufficient fuel to make it. We loaded up again and headed off, spending the rest of the morning riding across the desolate, semi-desert Pamir Plateau, the track making its way around small lakes, over high mountain ridges and through rivers. It was a joy of a morning, as good as, if not better than, the day before - if that could be possible. We had to stop often just to take in the vast, wild panorama of it, gently-sloping bowls of immense size filling the lower horizon while mountain range backing against yet another mountain range and then another surrounded us on all sides, the sky a dark indigo blue setting off the brilliant white of the clouds that were stacking above us. It was breathtakingly beautiful, one of the most isolated, remote and awe-inspiring landscapes I have ever seen. Other than one 4X4 that had passed on the track while we were setting up camp the night before, we had not seen a single other vehicle; that is one truck carrying cows and one 4X4 in thirty-six hours of travel, remote and wild and pure, the only signs of life an occasional eagle soaring on the thermals, a few rabbits and the gingery creatures that dig large holes all over the place that threaten to kill us if we were to hit one. (We found out later that they are Centinel Marmots - I think. But then, they could have been red or grey Marmots. Let's just call them Marmots. It doesn't matter. Whatever they're called, they still dig massive craters in the middle of the road - *that* matters.)

At times we lost the track and had to ride about a bit to find it again but the GPS kept us safe. We realised that, if it had snowed the night before, we would have been in serious trouble. The track crossed numerous small rivers and, in places, it was very muddy, so much so that at one point Gareth buried his back wheel to the hub in the mud and boulders. We managed to get the bike out by lying it on its side and filling the hole with boulders before we could continue. I took photos, of course, before helping him drag the beast out - to add to my "Gareth Getting Stuck on his KTM" collection.

We finally reached Shaimak at midday. According to Lonely Planet, Shaimak is a "strategic junction of the borders of Tajikistan, China, Pakistan and Afghanistan" but it looked like a dead and alive collection of dilapidated houses to me. We managed to get fuel decanted from a drum into a plastic container then to the tank, as is the norm in this far south eastern corner of Tajikistan. Very thirsty, we found a *Magazin* that sold stale, loose biscuits and "fruit" juice, which, in the 'Stans, contains 0.0001% fruit and enough sodium benzoate and food colourants to keep you buzzing for days.

Now for the "gosh awful"...

For rest of the afternoon we rode along one of the most shockingly corrugated dirt roads we have experienced on this trip. There were 122ks of this disgusting, bike-breaking, soul-destroying stuff that threatened to shake the bikes - and our brains - apart. There was little we could do about it - whether you rode in the car tracks, in the centre of the road or right on the edge, inches from the drop to the plain alongside, going fast or slow - *nothing* would help. We gritted our teeth and hammered on, wondering which parts of the bikes would fall off first.

After an hour or so, however, we discovered that the locals, also sick and tired of the beating their vehicles were taking, had simply decided to ignore the road and head off into the desert, making their own maze of tracks through the firm sand. We quickly left the main road and took to these tracks - which made for exciting riding, especially when we hit long stretches of bull dust, sudden right angle turns and a number of surprize dry river crossings which just appeared seemingly right in front of our wheels. But at least there were no rocks or corrugations.

Eventually, with Murghab only a few kilometres away, the road returned to passable tar... then Gareth ran out of fuel.

I had to leave him on the side of the road while I rode into Murghab, filled my container (by bucket) at a roadside garage and took fuel back to him.

Much later, very tired and dirty, we found our homely lodge where we were made welcome.

That night, looking at the map, Gareth was making noises about attempting part of the Bartang Pass, supposedly the gem of the Pamirs for bikers, the track very narrow with, in places, a cliff on one edge falling thousands of feet to the river below. It is one of the tracks we had marked as a *must do* (I wrote "Short cut - rarely accessed - landslides" on the map while I was planning possible routes before we left). Sadly, the Sary-Tash landslide had imposed severe time constraints on us but he thought we might be able to ride along half of it before doubling back and returning to the Pamir Highway then on to Sary-Tash and Osh. It would all depend on his bike - its lack of power at altitude, its fuel consumption, as well as the condition of the track and the availability of fuel. If we could manage that, then the only track we would not have attempted from our initial planning would be the Shokh Draa Valley north of the Wakhan Corridor.

Russian bikers

Shortly after setting off from Murghab, I glanced to my left and saw a mountain that seemed designed especially for stupid motorcyclists who should know better to attempt to ride up. The whole mountain seemed to be made of gravel with a smooth slope all the way to the top, something you look at and think: *With a bit of speed, I could get a fair distance up that!*

I accelerated level with Gareth and pointed. I could see him smile behind his visor as he immediately slowed and pulled off the road. The desert surface that led to the gently sloping base of the mountain was smooth, firm sand. Gareth powered ahead of me and I paused to watch him keep going, a plume of dust kicked up behind, up and up until he was just a small dot pinned against the side of the mountain. He'd got about three quarters of the way up.

Now it was my turn. Just under the firm surface, the ground was soft so the only way to keep momentum was speed. And with my bike fully loaded, speed is what I just couldn't get. The KTM 990 had the extra power needed to rise on to the firm crust; I tried it in second but the back wheel started digging in as soon as the slope steepened. I broke off for a longer run-up and only made it a tad further. I tried twice more, using various gears but made little impression. In the end, I gave it up and waited for Gareth to turn his bike on the very steep slope about 1000ft up and ride back down, the small dot of his bike being identified first by a plume of yellow dust that rapidly increased in size until he came hurtling past me, unable to stop. When he had turned and ridden back to me, he explained that he couldn't slow the bike - touch the back brake and the wheel slid sideways on the loose surface, too much pressure on the front brake would have had him tumbling head over heels down the mountain.

Jollies over, we headed off again along a very good tar road which continued along the high plateau between the mountains, vast blue lakes and shallow bowls that stretched across the horizon.

For many miles we rode alongside a barbed wire fence, head height with a T-piece across the top to deter people climbing over and I realised that this was the Chinese border. Whether the fence was there to keep the Chinese out of Tajikistan or to keep the Tajiks out of China I have no idea, but its effect as a deterrent was somewhat negated by the ragged holes that one could see periodically, ripped through the fence. One would have thought that the mountains alone were a sufficient barrier.

Once again we were travelling through an almost desolate landscape, although the good tar road gave it a semblance of civilization. All morning we had passed just one truck and there were no villages or even yurts with their shepherds and flocks of sheep to be seen. It was just too high for vegetation to flourish and the landscape on either side of us was desert, the harshness of the land softened a little by the high altitude coolness. Countryside of such austere beauty one would imagine would be a magnet for tourists but even the lakes, which in any European country would be dotted with sails and holidaymakers frolicking about in boats, were lonely in their stark isolation.

The highlight of the morning was when we came round a corner to see four or five bikers clustered around a downed motor bike near the edge of a lake just off the road and two people in biking gear hurrying towards us, waving and flagging us down.

We stopped to see whether we could help. Two Russian bikers approached us and the one, a young woman named Katya who spoke good English, asked whether we could help them - one of their group riding a heavy GS1200 had rather foolishly decided to investigate the lake and had ridden straight into deep, claggy mud - and then fallen over. There were six of them, four guys and two girls, all with their own bikes, heavily laden, bits strapped willy-nilly all over, spare fuel, spare road tyres (some of them had fitted knobblies at the start of the Pamirs and carried their road tyres with them) on a road trip from Moscow.

(I call him "foolish" but I suppose he was merely doing what Gareth and I had done earlier in the day - attempt to ride up the side of a mountain. If one of us had tumbled head over heels with our limbs getting minced up with parts of the bike, passers by would probably have called us foolish as well. It's a "challenge" when it works out; you're "an idiot" if it all turns pear-shaped.)

We walked with Katya and the other Russian down to the edge of the lake where the GS was lying, its one pot deeply embedded in the mud. They couldn't move it, even though they had stripped it of its luggage and had tied straps to the bike, using them in an attempt to pull it out. Now, with eight of us available, we grabbed hold of the straps and literally dragged the heavy GS out onto firm ground, its left pot digging a deep trench in the mud. We helped pick the bike up, caked with a thick layer of glutinous, yellow mud and Peter, the owner, started it up and rode it out, back onto the road.

Lesson No. 1: *Don't try to ride a heavy, laden bike through deep mud. It sinks.*

A week after we got back, Katya emailed us, attaching some photos. This is what she wrote:

Hello from Russia (crazy Russians from Karakul Lake)

Hello Gareth and Lawrence!

Happy to greet you!

How are you doing? Where are you both now?

So...I will let you know about all our adventures after we separated.

You remember Peter who nearly drowned his GS 1200? (That was his first whim!) That day we got to Osh city and next morning we went to Issyk-Kul lake through Djalal-Abad and Naryn. That time we didn't know that there will be two passes. The first pass was rather difficult - height about 3200 or 3500 and rapid ascents. We hardly passed 250 km for the whole day. In Kasarman village we decided to have dinner and stop for a night (so that not to go to the second pass at sunset), but Peter fell on completely level road (but there was deep gravel) on high speed, broke his arm and his motorcycle. Fortunately there was a hospital and even an X-Ray equipment at that God forsaken place! He looked very bad really... but the doctor said he had only an abarticulation and very little fracture so they put a bone into joint again and put an arm in plaster. No operation!

We called for the evacuation truck and next day Peter and his moto went to Almaty. From Almaty Peter went to Moscow by plane.

What about us - we successfully got to Issyk-Kul lake, then to Bishkek and Almaty and further to Russia. Now we are in Moscow.

Next time when you are in Moscow, please contact us, you can stay at our place.

Katya

Lesson No. 2: *Don't stuff around in the Pamirs - it can bite you in the bum when you least expect it.*

And then, a week later:

Hello Gareth!

Peter is ok, 2 days ago he got his motorcycle from Almaty (by track), now he will be repairing it.
Say hello to your dad!
Now we are in Sri Lanka, going to safari.

Regards,
 Katya.

For the rest of the day we rode with the Russians in an incidental rather than planned way - there is only one road and we were all heading in the same direction - stopped at the same cafe for lunch where they helped us order in Russian. Finally we reached the Kyrgyzstan border, rode to the top of the Torguart Pass and partly down the other side where we came to the landslide cutting. Bull dozers were still at work clearing the road of thousands of tons of rock that had blocked our way two weeks before. Since then they had managed to open a track just wide enough for one truck to pass through at a time. It was only as we rode through that it became clear just how large the landslide had been: Rocks had completely filled a good fifty metres of the cutting.

Now the road was running red with muddy water which had, in places, dragged a number of smaller rock slides down onto its surface, sometimes almost blocking it. Clearly, just before we had reached the pass, heavy rain had fallen and the Kyzyl-Suu river, which runs alongside the road down the pass, was in flood. We made our way carefully down the Alay Valley, thirty kilometres of downhill meanders, the road running with water and covered in rocks until, at last, we reached Osh and found a hot, crummy home-stay.

I was very tired, hot and sweaty. All I wanted to do was drink copious amounts of water, have a shower, consume a cold beer and collapse onto my bed. But the heavy-duty zip ties holding up my broken exhaust had again sheared and the silencer had been bashing against the brake calliper every time the rear suspension compressed. I needed to secure my exhaust pipe before it did any more damage or broke off altogether so I unbolted my pannier rack to gain access and strapped the exhaust back into place using a piece of wire I had picked up on the side of the road the previous day (just in case), a piece of washing line I "borrowed" from the property next door and, just to be certain the exhaust would not break free again no matter what the condition of the roads, my cable lock.

It was past nine before I was finished and darkness was setting in (although it did nothing to ameliorate the heat).

Before turning in that night, I wrote in my journal:

There comes a time in any traveller's life when he pauses for reflection and asks himself: Why?

It's getting dark, the temperature is hot enough to roast a chicken, you are up to your elbows in oil and there's sand in your hair; your bum itches, insolent flies drink moisture from the corners of your eyes, your stomach is tightening and coiling in that ominous way that signals the imminent evacuation of all your intestines from your rectum; your bike is falling apart bit by bit and you're not sure whether it's going to get you home before the last piece falls off; your nose is blocked with cement and whenever you blow it, it bleeds. Your body stinks. Your eyes are gritty. The last drop of water you've got is warm and you dare not attempt the water from the tap in your unspeakable bathroom in case it kills you.

Filled with self-pity, you plaintively ask yourself: Why am I here? What am I doing in this place? *I could be at home, right now, sitting in my comfortable chair with a cat on my lap and a cold beer in my hand, watching Moto GP on the telly or Charlie and Ewan doing their thing instead of me (with a 4X4 back-up truck, of course, and film crew just out of sight so we all think they're doing it alone and their fancy aluminium panniers are full of tools, spares, food and water and other essential stuff that's not tucked away safely in the 4X4).*

But then, as darkness begins to fall and the piece of wire you pulled from the fence and the clothes line you cut from the yard next door have been tightened and your exhaust is so well secured you know it will never fall off even if hit by an avalanche; you're rather pleased with yourself and your backyard mechanics, your boer maak 'n plan, *and you've had a cold shower in your hot room and got most of the grease off your arms and all the dust out of your hair and the flies have gone to sleep for the night and you've changed your clothes. Later you find some little smoky bistro down a side alley that sells cold beers and, quite coincidentally, at the same place are a couple of intrepid cyclists with stories to tell and a twenty-something young woman hitching from Katmandu to Marrakesch or Ulan Batour or Timbuktu or Tashkent - some exotic-sounding destination - and she smells like a woman should and looks great and you know she sees your grey hair and grizzled beard and wrinkles as signs, not of age, but of untold wisdom and experience - and suddenly you* know *why you're here...*

The joys of hospitality

Gareth fell ill.

A combination of gyppy tummy, the heat and probably dehydration had knocked him down.

We lay in, too tired and hot to contemplate packing up. I went out into the streets and bought a melon which we had for breakfast.

Eventually we got ourselves going and spent a fruitless hour battling our way through heavy, chaotic traffic in the oppressive heat, looking for a garage that might be able to rectify the KTM's faulty sensor. In the end we gave up and headed out of Osh on the road to Bishkek. Again, because of the absurd border demarcation of the 'Stans during the Soviet period, we had to make a long detour to prevent ourselves entering Uzbekistan, for which we had no visa.

The lowland around Osh is an urban sprawl, dirty and congested and unbelievably hot. Throughout the day, Gareth's bike registered an ambient temperature of 40C while we were riding, an oppressive, draining, debilitating heat that sucks the life out of you. About thirty minutes out of Osh, Gareth suddenly pulled off the road into a garage forecourt, stripped off his helmet, jacket and gloves and collapsed on the raised concrete plinth, white in the face.

"I just had to stop," he muttered. "I thought I was going to pass out."

We found two chairs used by the forecourt attendants and Gareth slumped in one of these, pulled his boots and riding trousers off and rested for half an hour.

Much later, cooler but still not feeling well, he stood up shakily and said he was able to continue, which we did until, in the late afternoon, we reached the town of Karakol. The whole day had been one of those grit-your-teeth-and-bear-it rides, the land flat and hot and dusty, uninteresting and stupefyingly hot. Fortunately, 30ks before Karakol, a large range of mountains appeared in front of us and the road began to climb. This didn't reduce the temperature by any significant degree but it varied the scene.

The Kyrgyzs have dammed the Sirdayro River in a number of places up a narrow gorge, the water a clear, turquoise blue; the road climbs into the Fersana Range of mountains, an impressive barrier across an otherwise flat landscape, made up of dark rock, unlike the sandstone ranges further south. Both the Kurp-Say and Toktogul Reservoirs, formed by the dammed river, are huge, the former (and smaller) continues up the steep river valley for over thirty kilometres and has, at intervals, a number of impressive hydro-electric installations.

Eventually, after a hard day's ride, we found a hotel in the town of Kara-Balta so typically ex-Soviet that it could have been a caricature. In fact, I proposed to Gareth the idea of travelling around Russia and ex-Soviet states where Russian architectural vandalism had been perpetrated, taking photographs and publishing a coffee-table book called: "Russian Bathrooms - an Overview" or some such catchy title. If Kevin Beresford can publish a photo book entitled "Roundabouts of Great Britain", then I can do one on Russian toilets. (By the way, "Roundabouts of Great Britain" can be purchased on Amazon from eighteen retailers for £0.01. I just checked.)

Still in our riding gear, wilting in the heat, we were confronted in the vestibule by that stolidly rotund, middle-aged woman who has been the backbone of Russian society for generations. She could have successfully commanded a camp in the Gulag during the purges. Looking at us suspiciously, she demanded, *"Passpirt!"*

Frustrated and hot, I remonstrated with her, indicating our state of distress and she relented (but without a smile) showing us our room. On a small table was a teapot but no kettle - I suppose it functioned as an ornament. When I asked her whether we could eat later and buy water now, she shook her head and made walking motions with her fingers and pointed towards the nearby village.

Ah, the joys of hospitality in an ex-Soviet hotel!

Gareth had a cold shower and collapsed onto his bed. It worried me that the whole of the Kazakh steppe - which we think will take us six days to cross - would be just as relentlessly hot and debilitating.

That night we toyed with the idea of travelling at night to escape the heat during the day across the Steppes. (And the police).

We will see.

Ghengis Khan dolls

Gareth still sleeping off his illness from the previous day, I got up the next morning and set off on my bike to buy another melon for our breakfast. Its moist coolness is all we can think about consuming in the muggy confines of our room.

Later, while we were packing up, our delightful hostess demanded the key to our room and physically checked that we hadn't stolen the towels before she returned our passports.

We then headed north from Kara-Kol along a good tar road through the lowveld heat, stopping briefly at the entrance to the hydro-electric power station just out of town (but guards at the gate wouldn't let us through). They were very friendly, though, and asked whether we would pose with them for photographs.

Soon after the road had made a massive, forty kilometre loop around the eastern edge of the Toktogul Reservoir, we began to climb and, from then on until we reached the outskirts of Kara-Balta, just west of Bishkek where we stopped for the night, the ride was delightful: it wound its way in a series of exciting switchbacks up and over the Suusamyr-Too mountain range via the Ala Bel Pass followed almost immediately by the Too-Asbuu Pass rising to 3586m, all in the delightful Goldilocks temperature of mid-summer high altitude, bracing but not cold. The scenery was spectacular and made me feel, for a while, that we were travelling through the territory of a rather down-on-his-luck second cousin of Switzerland. The mountains were intermittently snow-covered, the streams running next to the road small and crystal-clear, unthreatening bubbling brooks; at intervals, local bee keepers had arranged their multi-coloured hives alongside the road and sold bottles of clear honey from small, quaint stalls - so close to the hives that it was possible to eat the honey of the bee that just stung you. And then there were the yurts and herds of elegant horses ranging freely on the mountain slopes, herds of sheep grazing nearby so close that the pleasantly rank stench of their dung filled the air. Clearly the traditional yurt-dwelling Kyrgyzs prefer the mountains to the plains and seeing the round, white yurts erected next to clear streams with their flocks and horses is an image that will remain with me long after I have left this place.

Sadly, though, because this road cuts through such beautiful scenery and is on the main route from Bishkek south to the interior of Kyrgyzstan and Kazakhstan, it has become a favourite for tourists, and the yurt-dwelling Kyrgyzs have cottoned on to the fact that tourists = dollars; in a number of places they have set themselves up alongside the road for hundreds of metres, all with their rickety little stalls, all selling exactly the same things - milk stored in used plastic Coca-cola bottles and round, white sweets. Nothing more. Already litter is accumulating and the place looks tawdry and cheap. It won't be long before Made-in-China plastic camels, yurts encased in snow-storm plastic domes and glow-in-the-dark Ghengis Khan dolls are lined up for sale.

The tourist rot is setting in. I understand that people need to make a living but it makes me sad when I see an otherwise proud people reduced to sitting all day on the side of the road, their meagre offerings open to scrutiny and the whim of a tourist opening his wallet.

We finally turned onto the main Bishkek - Tashkent road and, as we need to head more west across Kazakhstan, it seemed unnecessary to travel the extra 68ks to Bishkek only to retrace our steps the next day. With six thousand kilometres to get home, who wants to add an unnecessary 136?

The banja

So, it was 4.30 and we needed a place to stay. After faffing about for half an hour mistaking first a dentist surgery and then a cafe for a *gostinitza,* we were directed to our present abode for the night.

It is, you may say, interesting.

The previous night's ex-Soviet monstrosity was, I recall writing, almost a caricature, a stereotype. Well, this hotel was the *real* deal!

From the outside it looked like a place where the KGB kept files on people they didn't trust (like everyone in the world), with an underground section, sound proofed, where they did things to you with pliers, live electric wires and hose pipes. Impressive on the surface in a bold style I would call *Rectangular Soviet Chic* (the interior, as we would soon discover, was impressive in an entirely different way).

Outside the hotel, a woman with two missing front teeth (the next two in line were gold, as if to make up for the missing ones) was smoking a roll-up with a man who looked like a tramp. They shouted something unintelligible at us and grinned their gappy teeth in welcome. Even from inside my helmet I could smell the tobacco and alcohol on their breath and oozing from their pores.

Gareth ventured in while I remained with the bikes. He emerged a few minutes later, laughing. "They want money first!" he told me, then added, "This is the worst hotel I've ever seen in my *life!* You pay! You pay *now!*" he mimicked.

It was *so* bad that we decided to ham it up, taking pictures of Gareth giving a cheesy grin and a thumbs-up at the prison-like entrance, the weed-covered back door and - ta-da! - our room!

We handed in our passports (you can't do anything in these places without relinquishing your passport which gives them total control of your life). Once they have your documents you can't steal the towels or toilet paper or do anything naughty; in fact, without your passport in this place you may as well go out and shoot yourself in the head.

Our delightful hostess Olga (probably) showed us where to park our bikes round the back of the building, which looked even more threatening than the front - all concrete right angles and rusting reinforcing rods, unpainted walls, peeling plaster and weeds.

A short while later we heard a commotion from the front of the hotel. Two local policemen were locked in a verbal battle with the bull-dog at the desk. We learned later that the policemen shared our suspicions that our bikes, left where they were behind the hotel, would no longer be there in the morning. In Russian, they made us understand that there were drunk people about and the bikes weren't safe.

So it was the policemen vs the bull-dog at the front desk. They wanted the bikes parked inside the hotel foyer for the night; the bull-dog said, *"Nyet!"*

The bull-dog won.

A compromise was finally reached and the bikes were pushed into a lower stairwell; our delightful hostess then selected a large key and led us into the dark bowels of the hotel to our room.

Come - please - join me as we walk through the dingy, concrete stair well, along a gloomy corridor covered with worn, puke-brown linoleum flooring (careful where it's lifted there; don't trip). I apologise for the darkness in the passage but - as you can see - none of the original neon light fittings work any more. The wires hang out of them like severed intestines but two have been connected to incandescent bulbs which hang down from the ceiling at about head height. But, sorry, they don't work either.

The lady - I use this term loosely, you understand - stopped outside a door. It seemed that someone had tried to light a fire in the corridor outside our room in the not too distant past because the linoleum was all charred and stained - to keep warm in mid-winter when the plumbing froze, perhaps. She gave Gareth the key but he, despite being an engineer, was unable to open the door. At some point in its history the blue-painted door had obviously been kicked in - both it and the frame showed signs of splintering that had been roughly patched with plywood. Eventually Gareth gave up and handed the key to the lady who, with a deft twist of her large arm and a kick, managed to turn it in the lock and get the door open.

Now, do come in - allow me to show you around our room. Yes, I know it's bland and nondescript, but it's a room you will find in a hundred thousand equally nondescript ex-Soviet and Soviet hotels wherever they have perpetrated their insult to comfort and decor. Notice the tasteful blue-painted doors and door-jambs; a notice tacked onto the inside of the bathroom door has also been painted over with blue but you wouldn't be able to read it anyway. Dirty green-flecked wallpaper; a musty smell - shall we open a window? No, sorry, the windows don't open but this one's broken so it will let fresh air in.

To your immediate right is the bathroom. As you can see, water constantly runs into the toilet bowl; cigarette butts in the water but no toilet seat or paper. Oh, you expected a toilet seat and paper? Silly you! There is no lid on the cistern and all the workings are visible but that makes it easy to flush if the handle breaks - just reach your hand into the water and lift the plunger thingie. A ragged hole in the floor serves as a drain. Five empty one-litre bottles are stacked in one corner. Please be aware of the empty electric sockets with bare wires covered with a single layer of Sello-tape. Don't worry - it's quite safe because there's no water in the shower pipe. But I seriously recommend that you don't stick your fingers anywhere near those wires coming out of the wall, OK? Note the chunky Soviet plumbing, the basin hanging off the wall. You will have seen, I'm sure, that the same tasteful shade of blue as the door has been used to paint the pipes, including the pieces of wire that hang from them above the grimy, rust-stained bath. Try the taps - oh, I beg your pardon, there's no water. Probably for the best - sitting in that bath could be seriously injurious to our health what with the bare wires hanging out of the wall...

Now, the bedroom: two narrow beds, one wardrobe without hangers or hanging rail - just an empty space. We can put all our biking gear in there. Tatty lace curtains, blue-painted window frames; one broken window. From the ceiling hang two overhead light fittings with tasteful '30s style glass covers, only one of which has a bulb, but we should be able to see with just the one. In one corner, a small table. For chairs, square pieces of chip-board have been placed loosely on top of wooden legs. Yes, there is a towel provided. See, on one of the beds is a small piece of threadbare material, one foot by two - well, I assume it's a towel. And, as there's no water, I suppose one can't complain...

Which reminds me, I need to find somewhere to wash so do excuse us. Can you find your own way out in the dark?

Thank you.

I must pause here for a moment: Realising that some of our Russian biker friends might read this account, I felt a little guilty about constantly knocking bad Russian architecture, hotels, bathrooms and toilets; perhaps they would feel hurt at my insensitivity. I emailed Sasha (who met us on the side of the road and encouraged us to join the Black Bears on their trip to Archangel a few years before), sent him my description of the hotel and said I hoped he wouldn't think I was being overly critical of his beloved Motherland.

This was his reply:

"At least the tile on the walls :) It's not so bad :)"

And then later he emailed:

"I know. And I totally agree. I mean I saw Russian hotels much worse than this one. In Sochi I had been staying at the hotel for a week, and it was dirty room as in check in day and while whole week as well, nobody tried to clean the room. It cost 60€ by the way..."

We were the only guests (well, the only ones stupid enough to go there, I suppose) so we went exploring: The second floor was all locked up. We climbed further; the third floor corridors were covered with a thick layer of dust, bird droppings and abandoned nests. Windows had been broken. Gareth was looking for a souvenir from the old Soviet days so, when we came across a metal ladder leading up to a trapdoor in the roof, we climbed up and peered through only to surprise a number of pigeons roosting in the roof space. They flew out of gaps with a clatter of wings leaving a haze of dust from the inches of bird droppings that covered the ceiling.

Like the Stygian tunnel, this place was so bad it made one want to laugh: dusty, dirty, run down, dilapidated, falling apart, depressing. No wonder people need to be drunk here to survive. No wonder Stalin chose places like this to send his political prisoners to exist and work and die. A sad place, full of people desperately trying to make a living, to survive - and I know it's wrong to come in from the outside and mock and judge, but, really, it was so bad that it's difficult not to.

Anyway, back to our room. Feeling hot and dirty, I pointed to the broken pipes and asked our Gulag Commander - with washing gestures - how I could have a shower.

She shook her head and pointed somewhere through the wall.

I made even more exaggerated washing motions saying, *"Douche? Douche?"* (Not knowing the Russian word for "shower", I made use of the French and hoped she would understand.)

She flashed her gappy gold teeth at me insisted, *"Banja! Banja!"* again pointing through the wall.

Now I had a vague knowledge that a *"banja"* was some kind of bath, perhaps one of those pine-scented rooms you find in Sweden, draped with blond, semi-naked Swedish women in their late twenties, swathed in fluffy white towels (or not, as the imagination dictates), red-glowing, pebble-smooth rocks in the middle and a stylish pitcher of water, placed to one side with due regard to *feng shui*.

Just swap the blond, Swedish twenty-somethings with Russian women in the imagination - *Yes, I could do that...*

Gareth and I went outside and looked. All we could see was the detritus of degrading concrete. (The alcohol-smelling man and woman had left.)

Sticking my head inside the foyer again, I asked, "Where?" making beckoning gestures and walking with my fingers.

Reluctantly she came outside with me, pointed and insisted, *"Banja!"*

There was a raised concrete manhole without a cover in the direction she was pointing, metal steps leading somewhere underground but clogged with litter. As it was in the hotel grounds and there was still no sign of a *banja* anywhere, I asked facetiously, pointing, "In here?" but with a smile so she knew I was only joking. (You don't want to upset a hefty, middle-aged, Russian-speaking woman with gold teeth, trust me.)

She came forward a few steps, still pointing.

Again I encouraged her to walk with us, using my fingers and a becoming smile - because, for the life of me, I could see nothing that looked vaguely like a *banja* in the hotel grounds. But she pointed back to the hotel entrance and said something like, "I'm terribly sorry, sir, I can't come any further with you, I'm responsible for this respectable establishment and someone might steal the towels."

In the end we got it. The *banja* wasn't in the hotel grounds at all - it was across the road. This delightful establishment not only served no meals, no drinks but, also, had no washing facilities whatsoever. If you wanted a bath or shower, you went across the street.

A large rectangular concrete building - *Soviet Chic* in style - squatted alongside the road with *BANJA* in Cyrillic letters across the front. We crossed the street to investigate. Inside the entrance was a large, empty, undecorated space covered with brown ceramic tiles; set into one wall was a small metal grill; behind the grill, a woman.

We mimed taking a shower and said, *"Douche?"* but she insisted,

"*Nyet - banja -*" and pointed to a card with a printed tariff of fees. Evidently, for $2 each we could enter and do whatever one did in there.

In an adjoining bare room, a few young women lolled about on wooden benches and Gareth commented that the *banja* probably doubled as the local brothel.

Having found the place and badly needing a wash, we went back to the hotel and got our soap and towels. On entering again, Gareth noticed that he could have his hair cut for $1 so off he went, leaving me to face whatever was behind the door on my own.

He told me later that a woman with a "dodgy eye", early twenties, thin and wiry, went at his hair with blunt, battery-operated clippers. The batteries were flat and the clippers constantly jammed in his hair so she repeatedly had to change them to get the job done. Then came the cut-throat razor treatment - also blunt - and she managed to rid his neck of unwanted hair by dint of pushing the blade very hard into his flesh and scraping.

But it was done in the end. He didn't mention whether she also offered him a "massage", but then he's private about these things.

Anyway, back to me. Clutching my towel and bar of soap, I opened a door and entered the contiguous room feeling very much like the new member of the golf club who doesn't know the rules. A young man came in with me to instruct me in the arcane rituals of the *banja*.

This second room, about three metres by ten, humid and airless, was floored with the same brown tiles as the entrance. The only furniture, a row of rather battered lockers and some wooden benches upon which were two naked men. The first was small and almost hairless - bald head, bald torso, almost bald pubes, thin string of a penis hanging between his legs; the other, almost by deliberate contrast, was large and hairy. He reclined on one of the benches lengthwise, like a male nude posing for a portrait, chest like a gorilla's, hirsute face, dangly bits... well, dangling.

For any of my female readers, men do this, I'm afraid. If we've got clothes on, we impress by the car we drive, the clothes we wear, gold chains, money, etc. But when we are all naked in a room together the only thing to compare is the size of our willies.

It's a man thing.

You hear stories of men with small tassels who hide whimpering in change room corners, shamed by their inadequacy while their more well endowed brothers strut about, flaunting their flagpoles and lording it over the flaccid inadequacy of those less kindly blessed.

I'm sure women do something similar but for the life of me I don't know what it is.

Anyway, these two naked men were chatting amicably and nodded a silent greeting to me.

My young helper pointed to the wooden lockers against the wall and indicated I should take my clothes off and put them inside; he would then lock them in (showing me a key) and, when I wanted them again, I was to push a button on the wall and he would come and unlock my locker. (All very Soviet. Why not just give me a key?)

Now naked, my clothes locked away and my helper gone with the key, I entered room No. 3. *Dante's 3rd level?* came to me briefly as I opened the door to an even larger and hotter room. I felt as if I were breathing hot water and wondered if I might drown in the air. Another naked man stood before a concrete block, about navel height, soaping himself.

The floor was mostly smooth terracotta tiles but filled in with cement where these had broken and come away. In the centre of the room was a drain hole partially plugged with gunk and hair, smelling like your drains do when they've been blocked for so long that your wife threatens to leave unless you call a plumber.

The naked man was using a black plastic bucket to slosh water over his head and body from taps attached to the concrete block. I looked around through the steam and saw a number of these buckets lying about so, following his example, I took one, set it down on another concrete block (there were about twelve, each supplied with two pipes with lever spigots). I felt each pipe to find the hot one, filled my bucket and, hoping it wouldn't kill me, quickly poured the contents over my head as I had seen the hirsute man do. It was so hot it took my breath away.

I soaped myself all over, breathing in the liquid air like a fish drowning.

I filled the bucket again with hot water and sluiced myself again... and again... and again. It was a strangely erotic experience.

Knowing that if you're Swedish or Russian or from northern climes, you're supposed to leap into an ice-covered stream after being in a *banja*, I then filled my bucket with cold water and, taking a deep breath, poured it over my head.

Whooo! It took my breath away.

I filled the bucket with hot water again and dumped it over my head.

Whooooo!

Then cold.

Whooooooo!

I could get to like this!

My skin was beginning to pucker.

I glanced over at my hairy friend and he was scrubbing away at his skin with what looked like a strap full of nails. Well, plastic nails. Lying about the floor I saw several of these things but realising they were probably clogged with the dead skin of previous masochists, I decided I'd give that a miss.

At about that time I heard an ominous *Flap! Flap! Flap! Flap!* coming from another room. My immediate thought was that the sound, clearly involving naked flesh being beaten, had something to do with pain and eroticism. I looked about the steamy room and saw yet another door set into the wall. Glancing about to make sure that no one was watching, I tip-toed closer. The *Flap! Flap! Flap!* was clearly coming from behind that very door. Tentatively, I opened it a crack and peeped in.

The heat hit me in the face like a bully. I reeled back, gasping. But I had caught a glimpse of a narrow cell of a room, about three metres by five, a naked man sitting on the top rung of five wooden tiers, alternately beating his back and his chest with a bunch of leafy twigs.

I shut the door quickly. Whether it was the heat or the naked man, I'm not sure - probably both.

But if I was to experience the full joy of this *banja,* I knew I had to enter the Fourth Level, face it like a man. While I stood outside the door trying to pluck up courage, the flagellating man exited, leaving me alone.

Next to the door, I noticed some bunches of what looked like leafy oak twigs tied together with string (but which, now that I've looked it up, were probably birch - called a *vihta* in Finland, evidently.)

I told myself to man up. I can do this. I breathed deeply, screwed my courage to the sticking point, opened the door and stepped inside, closing it behind me.

The heat inside that dark, concrete cell was truly frightening. Determined to experience it fully, I made my way up the slippery wooden bleachers and sat down at the top. My head was close to the ceiling and I gasped, genuinely afraid that I might pass out. I suddenly became aware that I was sitting in something that could easily be a torture chamber; claustrophobic bare concrete seemed to press in upon me, compounding the effect of the damp heat that threatened to drown me, stifle me, overwhelm my senses. An image of water boarding came to mind. I was being water boarded without the use of a towel over my face.

But what was perhaps even more frightening (considering the exposed electric wires we had seen on the streets and in buildings throughout the 'Stans just waiting to kill anyone who ventured too close) was the loud buzzing sound coming from directly beneath the wet, wooden bleachers, emanating from some massive, primitive source of electricity being used to heat this awful place, so powerful that one would imagine the lights of Kazakhstan dimming and flickering when it's fired up. Gareth said it reminded him of something alive hiding in the dark beneath him. And to think that everything was wet, us, the floor, the wood, condensation dripping from the walls and ceiling and right there, in the room, underneath where we were sitting, was enough electricity to electrocute the entire world buzzing loudly to itself, waiting...

Frightened I might die in there and that Gareth would come in after his hair cut and find my par-boiled/electrocuted body sprawled on the concrete floor, I gave myself some tentative blows across the back and chest with my *vihta* and then whimped out, making my way carefully down the wet, slippery bleachers and then out into Room 3, which felt positively cool by contrast. Gritting my teeth, I filled a bucket with cold water and quickly poured it over my head.

Whooooo!

Gareth walked in. With his shaved head, thin naked body and the blue and white striped plastic covering on some tables, I caught a disturbing image of Jewish prisoners in Belsen, stripped and shaved, lining up outside a gas chamber. I initiated Gareth to the rigors of Room 4, then left him to cook on his own while I poured a few more buckets of water over my head. When he emerged, equally fearful for his life, I pushed the buzzer to be released. Our helper emerged and unlocked the lockers. We dressed and emerged like troglodytes into the sunshine, our flesh clean and tingling.

An alcohol-smelling, toothless woman latched onto us the moment we entered the outside foyer and dragged us off to a "cafe" situated just behind the *banja*. She led us through a door into a back yard filled with junk, piles of cardboard, broken children's toys, a dead car on concrete blocks and other waste.

At a table, a woman was stuffing sheep's intestines with meat to make sausages; in a basin next to her, a sheep's stomach stank.

We thanked her politely but decided we would not patronise her establishment for our meal that night...

Later that evening, when the air had cooled a little, we walked out to look for a cold beer only to be met by our two friendly policemen outside the front of the hotel, escorting a diminutive man, drunk and unsteady on his pins, towards the police van to enjoy his night in the cells.

It was still too hot to eat so we bought a melon for breakfast and a selection of fruit for our supper from a roadside stall which we consumed later in our room.

When we returned, the Bull-dog was waiting for us. She beckoned us, stony-faced, down to the lower stairway where the bikes had been stored and pointed accusingly at some small pieces of concrete that Gareth had knocked out of the stairs when he rode the bikes up through the back door of the hotel. She was not impressed.

Gareth apologised. He told me he wanted to buy them flowers just to see if he could make them smile.

Later she dragged the policemen to the back of the hotel and pointed out the incriminating pieces of concrete. They looked suitably chastened.

As soon as they were gone, Gareth tip-toed down the stairs and got rid of the evidence.

Bad roads again

The next morning early, the Gulag Commander arrived at our room as we were packing up, walked in without a by-your-leave and demanded we give her the *klyuch*.

She didn't smile...

I have now experienced some of the best and worst of Kazakhstan's roads.

After some rain in the night and, also, perhaps a wind blowing from the south off the snow-capped Kyrgy and Ala-Too mountain ranges, the day began pleasant and cool. These mountains mark the border between Kyrgyzstan and Kazakhstan, almost as if the Kyrgyzs had first choice and claimed the mountains, leaving the hot, level plains for the Kazakhs.

At first, as we set off from Kara-Balta after enduring the painfully slow, third-world process of getting through passport control and customs into Kazakhstan, the road was brand new and silky smooth - so easy to ride that I found myself constantly battling to stay awake. That lasted much of the afternoon.

We thought, if the roads are like this all the way to the Russian border, we'll be across in a jiffy!

Then, as they always do, things changed. We reached the part where the old road was being turned into the new - trucks, graders, machines and dust plagued us for over an hour.

Where the old road was still functioning, it was hell: squashed, squeezed and pummelled, breaking up, pressed like a sponge cake into ridges and furrows by the tyres of massive trucks that had trundled their way across these plains for decades; even when it looked smooth, the bikes were being bounced and pounded constantly.

At about five thirty we arrived at Shymkent, a lovely modern town, and needed to stay at a posh hotel to get our passports registered. We tried three hotels and all had no rooms with twin beds, so Gareth and I cuddled up together in a double bed that night.

In reality, I wrote in my journal that night, *this is what the road is probably going to be like for the next three thousand ks. If it is, we are in for a torrid time. My head aches from being rattled and battered about all day. I shudder to think what it is doing to the bikes. It was like riding along a bad corrugated dirt road without the dirt.*

No dirt - well, I suppose that's one thing to be thankful for.

Steven Gerard and the Queen

Day two across Kazakhstan and I fell ill. I now know what Gareth felt like when he nearly collapsed on the side of the road a few days before.

We set off in the heat and it wasn't long before I vomited into my helmet. I just couldn't stop and get it off in time. Fortunately I had not eaten and had been drinking a lot of water so the result wasn't too disgusting.

After a long break sitting on the side of the road, recovering, I decided to attempt to soldier on. Feeling sorry for myself wasn't going to get us home any time soon. There were 160ks to the next town - Turkistan - and I felt I could make it. Just. In retrospect, it probably wasn't a wise decision. For some reason I couldn't focus my eyes; they kept collapsing inwards and I was seeing double, like when you try to look at your nose. I desperately wanted to sleep. Twice on that nightmare journey I did fall asleep but woke before I went off the road or hit anything. Gareth was leading and all I had to do was follow (and not ride into him). I could feel my eyes begin to lose focus, collapse inward and my brain would start to shut down. I would then try everything to keep focused and stop myself falling asleep: keep my visor up, stand up on the pegs, shake my head, bash my helmet with my hand, beat my head on the handle bars - nothing worked for long; I rode on automatic pilot. Whenever we came across a tree on the side of the road casting its pool of shade, I yearned to pull off and lie down, let go and sleep for a few hours, but the effort of trying to overtake Gareth and tell him was just too much. All I could do was grit my teeth and hang on, counting down the kilometres.

We finally reached Turkistan, booked into a hotel and I collapsed onto the bed and slept.

By late afternoon I was feeling more human and went for a walk into the mind-numbing heat, to have a look at the Yasaui Mausoleum, an impressive 14th century structure, the walls elaborately veneered in blue, white and turquoise tiles, with an eighteen metre diameter dome. It had been constructed using mud bricks but the builder, Timur, died before it was completed. One of the façades is still incomplete and bare of tiles, and centuries' old scaffolding poles still protrude from the walls. An important place of pilgrimage and worship for Sufi Muslims, it is believed locally that three pilgrimages to Turkistan are equivalent to one to Mecca.

As the evening cooled, Gareth and I walked about the town but I still felt ill; every exertion tired me and I was plagued with a constant thirst.

A drunk man joined us on the pavement, accompanying us and claiming loudly, "I love England! Steven Gerard... Margaret Thatcher... the queen! Respect!"

I'm sure the queen will be pleased to be placed third in line to Steven and Maggie in terms of respect.

You jokin' me, mate?!

The road leading north-west into the Steppes is followed on the right hand side by a low range of blue hills, shy and retiring and never coming close to the road as if just a little embarrassed that the highest peak in Kazakhstan reaches the staggering height of no more than two hundred metres. At some point during the morning the hills disappeared, leaving behind the flatness of the Steppe, hovering just above sea level at about 140m, sandy and parched like the dry bed of an ancient sea.

I didn't even notice its going.

To the left, according to the map and my GPS, the river Syr Darya drains massively from the Kyrgz mountains, making its way towards what's left of the Aral Sea. We crossed it only twice during the day, brown and slow-moving, nudging its way between sand banks.

At some point I noticed we had been joined by the rail line on its way to Russia; it ran alongside us, about two hundred metres away, as if it needed company. Two trains trundled slowly past us during the day going south, both long and carrying a mixed cargo in box cars, flat beds and liquid containers. The flatness of the land here must make constructing road and rail links easy and allow for very long trains.

Telephone poles stitched the landscape together, appearing out of nowhere and then disappearing into the haze of the opposite horizon. Occasionally we would come across a small town of clustered, dirty brown, unpainted houses like a scattering of cardboard boxes on the desert surface. And then there were the cemeteries built on raised ground like tiny hilltop villages in Italy, their onion domes and crenulated façades confusing the mind until true perspective returns and you realise that you are looking at a city in miniature, a crowded place of dead souls, each mausoleum built according to the wealth of those who remain, mostly just a crude brick courtyard three by two metres in size, sometimes surmounted by a crude, metal crescent moon, but others like small empty houses, up to twenty-five feet high, domed and intricately built, fit to honour the body of a wealthy man. If the Taj Mahal, the pyramids, the Shah-i-Zinda are mausoleums for the wealthy, for princes and pharaohs, then these are humble copies, tributes to the dead, small cities filled with their silent, spirit inhabitants.

The road, fortunately, at first, was good and we made steady progress north, slowly eating into the thousands of kilometres needed to cross this vast land.

As I rode, I tried to imagine, during the early days, travellers attempting to cross this seemingly endless Steppe when the road was just a dirt track. I can now understand why the Russians used parts of Kazakhstan to house their millions of political prisoners during the days of the Purges: if you escaped, there was simply nowhere to go - just impassable mountains to the south and three thousand kilometres of barren desert to the north. The heat would fry you in summer and the cold would kill you in winter. There was nothing you could do but make the best of it and hope the regime would change before you died.

About half died. Some historians put the number at ten million.

The road ran almost straight and the big sky overhead was a pale blue, as if most of the colour had been leached out by the heat.

I saw a lot of grass. Short and fine like the fur of a moulting camel; not what I had expected. Before I had seen it for myself, I had always pictured the Kazakh Steppes as vast expanses of yellow wheat, ready for harvest, across gently rolling plains to the horizon, the bread-basket of Central Asia; or grass, waist-high, rippling in the wind as far as the eye could see.

And yurts, obviously.

And sheepskin-clad men on horseback clutching bows and arrows...

(Like my mind's-eye picture of the Silk Road, I suppose - and just as romantically anachronistic.)

But the reality was significantly different: for most of the morning - about two hundred kilometres - there was no cultivation at all, just this very short, fine, tufty grass barely able to cover the ground which showed through as dry and sandy. In fact, one could imagine just a nudge more climate change, reducing the rainfall a few millimetres a year, the earth warming a degree or two more, and these Steppes would soon become the largest desert on earth. I had the feeling it was clinging on to the term "grassland" with its fingernails while the spectre of semi-desert crept ever closer.

During the entire day I saw a hundred sheep, ten cows, fifteen camels and forty horses. (Well, I'm guessing - I didn't actually count.)

I saw a rock.

This entire area is just sand, sparsely covered by a thin veneer of vegetation.

I saw fifteen trees.

In the early afternoon we came across the first of many large canals, dug during Soviet times to tap water from the Syr-Daraa, a massive, bold scheme termed the "Virgin Lands Campaign" but with many regrettable consequences. The best known is the drastic shrinking of the Aral Sea. They diverted so much water from the rivers that had previously flowed into the sea that evaporation quickly began to exceeded replenishment and the sea, once the world's fourth largest lake, covering 66,900 sq ks, began to shrink. Today the Aral Sea is pretty much dead, a fraction of its previous size and badly polluted from over fertilization of the surrounding land.

Salinization, so devastating to crops, was visible in the soil as we rode, large expanses of white salt deposits covering bare patches of land where water had evaporated from small depressions. Also, the method of irrigation seemed to me to be wasteful in the extreme: I observed no sprinklers anywhere in Kazakhstan; where land was irrigated, the crude and wasteful flood method was used, opening a sluice in the canal wall and flooding large expanses of land willy-nilly. But, from what I could see of the irrigated countryside through which we passed, the vast tracts of wetland created by this flooding has led to little more than a proliferation of very healthy, verdantly green but economically useless reed beds.

Lonely Planet puts it well and is worth quoting: "Central Asia's 'empty' landscapes served as testing grounds for some of the worst cases of Soviet megalomania. Land and water mismanagement and the destruction of natural habitat were part of a conscious effort to tame nature (*'harness it like a white hare',* as the propaganda of the day had it). The results are almost beyond belief and on a staggering scale.

"Even casual students of the region are familiar with some of the most infamous catastrophes of Soviet environmental meddling: the gradual disappearance of the Aral Sea and the excessive levels of radiation around the Semipalatinsk nuclear testing site. Add to this the consequences of Khrushchev's Virgin Lands scheme, which was planned to boost grain production but which ended up degrading tens of millions of hectares of Kazakh steppe..."

We planned to explore the dry lake bed west of Aral over the next day or so where the rusting hulks of large fishing vessels are supposedly to be seen on dry land, left abandoned as the water receded.

As the afternoon waned and clouds began to form in the pale sky, we left the area of flood-irrigated land and returned to the flat, semi-desert landscape of the Steppe. The new road was still under construction and, periodically, we had to divert onto shockingly rough sections of dirt, badly churned up by heavy trucks which trundled along at walking pace throwing up clouds of dust.

And, as our shadows lengthened, the land changed: imperceptibly, the grass died away to be replaced by sage and salt-bush. All traces of domesticated animals disappeared. This terrain could no longer be called grassland; in front of our eyes, in the space of just a few hours' riding, it had become semi-desert with patches of pure desert showing through the thin skin of hardy, drought-resistant vegetation that still managed to cling to life.

After a long day's ride of 450ks, we finally reached Baykonur (or Leninsk), the cosmodrome where Russia's space programme continues to flourish, where all Soviet and Russian-crewed space flights since Yuri Gagarin have taken place. As we rode towards the town, I kept looking at the sky in the hope of seeing a rocket being launched. But Gareth assured me that he'd checked on the Internet before we left and no launches were scheduled.

After the collapse of the Soviet Union, Russia negotiated a lease for a large tract of land around Baykonur for umpteen gazillian roubles a year so they could continue launching rockets into space. What is pleasing is that they are now involving the Kazakhs in the programme and in 1991, Toktar Aubakirov became Kazakhstan's first cosmonaut. But the whole of this area is, so to speak, Russian soil. This we found out when we rather naïvely attempted to enter the town, hoping to find a place to stay the night so we could visit the Russian space programme museum.

We duly joined a queue of vehicles stopped at a barrier manned by Russian guards. One was walking up the row of vehicles asking to see identity cards. Still we didn't get it. When he came to us, we showed him our passports but he just shook his head and walked on.

We parked the bikes, got off and made our way to the barrier, approaching a man who seemed to be in charge. We showed him our passports and asked if we could enter. He dug into his pocket and pulled out his identity card, asking us whether we had one.

We shook our heads.

And this is the first time I have ever come across a Russian official with a sense of humour. When we indicated that we didn't have the correct pass, he just smiled. But it was an indulgent, rather quizzical smile, the sort of smile that says, "You jokin' me, mate?! You want to get into a *Russian* space centre *without a pass? Hooo, boy!*"

Duly chastened, we turned away then rode about in the unbearable heat for half an hour looking for somewhere to stay. Eventually we asked a group of men and one gestured for us to follow him. He got into his car and led us to a nondescript *gostinitza* nearby. Most important: it had a cold shower. Granted, it was made from a water pipe with spigot, nailed to a beam above a piece of plywood on the floor; the rose rather cunningly constructed from a Coke can, holes punched in the bottom, attached to the pipe with wire - but it worked!

We asked our *gostinitza* proprietor whether she could provide us with a meal and she asked us to come back at seven and it would be ready, which we did. After we had eaten and wanted to pay, like a mother providing for her errant student offspring, she smiled and waved us away. No charge.

It's been strange travelling through Kazakhstan how we are treated as some minor celebrities. In the other 'Stans too. Everybody waves as we pass; children stand in the road and hold out their hands to be slapped as we ride by; everywhere we go we are greeted; people poke their heads out of car windows to call, *"Atkuda!"* - Where are you from? Sometimes, when people see us coming and have time, they whip out their mobile phones, lean into the road to snap us as we head past. When we stop, men and boys cluster around, staring at the bikes, commenting on the GPS, asking where we are going, how much the bikes cost, where we have come from.

We've seen no bikers or any travellers now for a week, not since we met the Russians with the bogged GS. We seem to be way out of the normal tourist routes here.

We rather like it that way.

Seeing that the "ship cemetery" is seventy kilometres along a small road angling more to the west than the main road, which then continues on for another 440ks, Gareth suggested we continue on this track rather than retracing our steps after we found the beached ships the following day. It sounded exciting but would take us to the limit of our range, even with full tanks and all three spare petrol containers.

That night I wrote in my journal, not knowing at the time just how prescient I would be: *I suppose it will all depend on what the road is like. Probably soft sand all the way...*

Racing the train

We left early while the sun was low and the air fairly cool, and made our way steadily across a desert landscape towards Aral, the road good, straight as a ruler, our shadows moving from in front of us to the side as the sun rose and made its way across a washed-out sky.

The terrain across which we made our way hour after long hour, stretching to the horizon on either side of us, was flat and barren, a landscape of nothing. The only life, a few camels that stood, alone and untended, staring with the timeless insouciance of its breed into the far-off distance.

At some indeterminable place and time during the day a lonely train trundled slowly past before disappearing into the heat-haze. Every fifty kilometres or so a wooden water tower would rise above the flatness of the land like a sentinel, relics of the old days of steam.

Occasionally, usually close to a pool of water, we passed small herds of horses, and I imagined them as leftover remnants of the sturdy mounts ridden by the Mongol hordes who swept over these plains, conquering all who opposed them. And that made me think of these Kazakh people, proud and free on their horses, ranging the semi-desert plains with their flocks of sheep, their camels, living the kind of itinerant life that had sustained them for generations. Being nomadic, they were able to control overgrazing and keep this vulnerable land fertile and productive. It was a delicate balance, maintained for centuries, sustaining a precarious lifestyle.

And then Stalin decided to tame the Kazakhs, turn them into obedient little Communists.

And so, one day, some faceless Soviet bureaucrat would arrive to tell them that, as of *now*, all their precious animals belonged to the state; they were now part of such and such a Collective, could no longer roam the Steppes looking for fresh pasture, but would be expected to form a sedentary community, till the land and start producing grain.

They called it *denomadisation*.

Furthermore, each Collective would be required to produce and supply X amount of grain each year to the state in accordance with the latest 5-year plan - and if it wasn't delivered, punishments would follow.

If they refused to obey, opposed being "collectivised" - as many did - they'd be shipped off to some god-forsaken Gulag or killed. And so, being the proud people they were, they slaughtered their flocks rather than hand them over to the state and, inevitably, were slaughtered themselves as punishment. Those who were left, those who submitted to *denomadisation*, struggled to farm this semi-desert land and, as most had already killed their animals, of course they starved. Hundreds of thousands died. And the Russians, under Stalin, let them starve as a punishment and a warning. After all, they had millions of Russian peasants who were crying out for land and could be resettled here.

So, the nomadic *free riders*, outlaws against any outside interference, became forcibly tamed, turned into bad farmers while the land was poisoned, topsoil blown away and the desert began to encroach.

Although no definitive number can put on it, it is believed that during 1929-53 eighteen million people passed through the Soviet labour camp system. About half of them died.

It was tragic to see it in the flesh, as it were, as we rode along. The ecological balance is so clearly teetering on a knife edge that it will take great statesmanship to turn it around. Because, sadly, this place is already well on its way to becoming a true desert.

Sobering reflections.

We reached Aral by noon and rode about aimlessly, looking for evidence of beached ships or the deep channel that was dug in a vain attempt to give their ships access to deeper water. We could see where the shoreline of the sea once existed, now dusty and clogged with litter. The town itself was dirty and sprawling and quietly wilting in the heat. Sand encroached onto the roads, blown in from the surrounding desert. It was hard to imagine that this was once a thriving fishing port, trawlers moored in deep blue water, ferries from across the sea docking and disgorging passengers. Now, where once there was water, sand and dust and litter seemed to define the town.

Eventually giving up, we filled our tanks and all spare fuel containers, giving us a range of about 420ks, which we hoped would be enough to get us through this stretch. We managed to buy some potatoes and sweet corn for our supper because we intended to camp out on the way, and headed out of town. It was good to be on the cusp of an adventure again after a number of pretty mindless days on a straight tar road. We had no idea what the road would be like or what we would encounter along the way but decided to give it a go in an attempt to find those iconic ships beached and stranded in the middle of the desert when the water dried up. We would be riding along the bed of the Aral Sea, so long gone that small settlements had grown up along the route of the rail tracks.

A few kilometres out of town we found the turn-off and followed a good but heavily patched and lumpy tar road and I thought, if this is what it's going to be like for the next four hundred or so kilometres, we'll be fine. But shortly afterwards we passed a large mining complex, the tar road died and reverted to dirt.

And then Gareth had another puncture. We removed the rear wheel and fitted my spare tube, baking under the blazing sun. Then on to a rail crossing where we asked the guard for directions. He pointed to the north west and said in Russian, "Go straight on. Don't turn to the left or right. Just go straight."

So, riding alongside one another, we began to follow this track, just two car tyres wide, deeply cut into the surrounding landscape so we were riding about six inches below the desert surface, each keeping to one wheel track. The ground was smooth and undulating with some patches of soft sand but always firm underneath and it was good to feel the response of the tyres on dirt again, the rise and dip of the wheels, the silky floating when you encounter soft sand. This was big trailie riding at its best, when you just *have* to stand on the pegs and feel the bike responsive between your legs, the wind pressing against your whole body, your added height giving a new perspective to the flat land. We kept on like this for at least eighty kilometres, stopping at two small villages along the way to ask about the stranded ships. Because we had difficulty communicating, we tore a page out of my journal and drew pictures of a ship on land, an anchor. (Gareth even drew some fish swimming about in the air above the ship, which must have confused them more than a little.)

They looked at our carefully drawn motifs with perplexed looks on their faces while we pointed first at the pictures and then this way and that in the surrounding desert saying, "Ships? Ships?"

They shrugged their shoulders, probably thinking, *Mad foreigners!*

We rode on, staring into the endless expanse of nothing that was once the bed of the Aral Sea. Then the wooden poles carrying telephone wires left us and we were alone in the desert with only the rail line and a few camels for company, following two sandy tracks.

But no ships.

Suddenly the track began to deteriorate into deep sand. Ugly, unpleasant sand. And riding along tracks in deep sand I find incredibly difficult. In the open it's not too bad because you just accelerate and let the front wheel find its way; but in a soft, narrow track sunk below the level of the surrounding land, unless you keep the front wheel *exactly* in the middle, it bites into one edge and immediately begins to slew from side to side. With a heavy load on the back accentuating the sway, I usually go down.

Which I did.

Gareth was ahead of me and didn't see me fall. I managed to pick the bike up and got it going again in the soft sand - memories of Morocco. I kept it up for the next two kilometres, fighting my way through, knowing that I wouldn't be able to keep it up for much longer in that heat. Another 330-odd kilometres - yeah, right!

The tracks dipped down a soft ridge, almost like an old dune, and I saw Gareth at the bottom, stopped. Ahead of us, blocking our way, was a large sand dune, forty foot high, covered with a sparse growth of vegetation. The tracks simply disappeared. Clearly, we weren't going any further.

Gareth climbed the dune to see whether he could see the road. On the other side of the rail line, he called down, there was a track but it looked like soft sand, just like this one.

We agreed that there was no way we could attempt such a long distance across terrain like that and turned around. To cross the three kilometres of sand on the way back, especially trying to get over the old dune we had ridden down, I decided to ignore the wheel tracks and make my way straight across the sand, which I found much easier.

A short while after we had regained the firm tracks, a long train trundled past us, heading in the same direction as we were. We waved to the driver - as you do - and he waved back.

Now what followed was, perhaps, one of the more memorable, and enjoyable, half hours of the whole trip. Gareth and I were riding alongside one another, each keeping to a wheel track so that neither of us had to ride in the other's dust. And as we rode, we became aware that we were, at about 50kph, keeping up with the rearmost coaches of the train whose driver we had waved to a short while before, a hundred or so metres ahead of us. Now there was no communication between us at all in what happened next; I don't know whether we simultaneously had the same idea, but it seemed that we both decided that we were going to catch that train. We were going to pass it. It was a challenge!

It didn't happen suddenly. Our speed increased slightly; we kept together, both standing, gripping the bikes with our knees, absorbing the dips and rises of the track. Slowly we started to gain on the rearmost coach. Over the next few minutes, it became a race - not against each other: *the train!* We didn't glance at each other, smile, make chasing gestures at all - just keeping the bikes on the narrow wheel tracks as they curved and undulated across the humped ground was difficult enough. We started to fly - 60kph... 70... then just nudging 80... still side by side, Gareth in one of the wheel tracks and me in the other, handle bars and panniers not more than a foot apart. There was an unspoken understanding between us, a tacit unity of purpose: *We were going to beat that train!*

As if tied together by an unseen rope, we mirrored each other as the tracks dipped and rose, twisted, split and rejoined, following the parallel depressions like Scalextric cars. Because the road had worn itself below the level of the land, we could use the raised edges like berms on the corners, both leaning together this way and that, the surface so smooth we could have been flying.

Of course we were going far too fast for the conditions of the track but it seemed, at that time, we bore charmed lives. Nothing could touch us. We were like naughty schoolboys getting up to mischief behind the bicycle sheds at school, wondering how long before we'd be caught, loving every illicit minute of it. Like a child on a fairground ride calling out to whoever would hear: *"More! More!"*

And there *was* more. It just went on and on until we caught up with the train and slowly passed coach after coach... and then we were neck and neck with the engine, racing across the dusty Kazakh Steppes, trying to imagine what the train driver was thinking but not being able to look or take a hand off the bars to wave. Finally we left it trundling along on its ponderous way behind us but we still kept up the speed, just on the edge of stupidity, feeling indestructible, leading charmed lives as we managed to clear the occasional obstacle, slow just sufficiently not to be catapulted over the handlebars by sudden dips then speed up again, hearing the tyres sing. At times one of us would be slowed by a branch across the track or a hidden dip or fly off onto the desert surface when we couldn't make a particularly tight corner or one of us would take a different set of the branching tracks and we would separate for a while before coming together again further along the way.

And as I rode, as if a part of my brain detached itself from the process of controlling the bike, switched on the autonomous nervous system so that the riding became a muscle memory, I became acutely aware of my son riding next to me, parallel to me, tied to me in some intangible way. It reminded me of the comment someone made who saw us riding across a section of Moroccan desert - *drifting together* - that, at the time, was so meaningful to me. For this brief time, racing the train with my son, my age seemed no longer to have any significance; my skill level on that road was equal to his; we rode together as one, father and son, but more than that: just two guys out having a jolly, doing what we love together and being somewhat irresponsible.

And, as our wheels flew across the firm sand and another part of my brain, the sensible part, warned, *Slow it down a bit, mate, you're riding on the edge here* and I replied, *Yes, I know, but I'm having such fun!* there was a part of me that wondered how long it would last: Not that track. Not racing the train. The travelling together, just the two of us.

I will continue to age and, eventually, my dwindling strength will become a hindrance. I wouldn't want Gareth to ride with me out of a sense of obligation.

But then, I thought, I can do it *now* and I will enjoy it while I can, however long it lasts. I've read of eighty-year-olds embarking on epic motorcycling trips so that gives me another... what?... seventeen years. So I'll take each year as it comes, each trip a blessing, live in the moment for a while longer and let the future go where it wills.

Suddenly the track deteriorated. I bottomed out hard a number of times, my engine scraping the ground; Gareth very nearly went over his handlebars when he came across a hidden dip in the road and *just* managed to slide to a stop as he hit it, bashing his face on his screen.

Our jolly was over; we'd raced and beaten the train. We'd had some of the best riding we'd ever experienced. We'd survived without breaking any bones. The bikes hadn't been destroyed...

Until about seven in the evening we rode on at a more sensible pace, a pace more in keeping with my years, you might say. It was still very hot and I was exhausted so I suggested we stop and camp for the night. There were no trees or clear, tinkling streams so we had to take what we could get - a dusty patch of desert, blindingly white in the sun, at the foot of a high, barren hill of eroded, white clay. As soon as we had stopped, I stripped off my riding gear and lay on my sleeping mat on the desert surface in the meagre shade of the bike, too hot and exhausted to set up camp, drinking water so warm that it could have come from a recently-boiled kettle. Nothing would quench my thirst. I decided to sleep under the stars that night. At least then I wouldn't have to put up my tent.

Much later, when the sun was lower over the horizon but the heat still blazed from the bare ground, we walked about picking up dried dung and small sticks and twigs, burned white from the sun, that lay about the desert surface so we could make a fire to cook our potatoes. How I longed for a cold shower, a cold beer, a watermelon!

We got a fire going just as the sun began to set. By now it was after nine. Our water was running low and we both still had thirsts that would not be quenched.

There was a village whose lights we could see about two kilometres away and, on a whim, I fired up my bike and headed straight across the desert to the village in search of water. After asking a few kids who were wandering the streets, I was directed to a shop whose owners opened up for me. They had a working fridge and I bought litres of ice cold water and lemonade. I was so looking forward to riding back to camp, telling a disappointed Gareth that there was nothing and then - *Ta, da!* - revealing my treasures.

I packed the bottles in my pannier, got on the bike, pressed the starter.

The engine turned over but it wouldn't start.

I tried again.

Nothing.

I spoke to God about it, using a reasonable tone.

Nothing. Completely dead.

I remonstrated with God, a little peeved now.

Nothing. Other than the starter motor, there was not a hint of life.

A group of little boys appeared. I called them over and asked them to give me a push, which they did with enthusiasm. Select second gear, stand, drop your weight hard onto the seat to give added traction to the back wheel, let go of the clutch... nothing.

I had a serious conversation with God about then, holding back my frustration, explaining that I would now have to walk at least two kilometres into the desert, try to find our camp, hope I wouldn't get lost, be very late with Gareth getting worried, and my little surprise of producing six litres of ice cold water and lemonade would be ruined. I contemplated making a bargain: God, if you just let the bike start this one time, I'll... but I didn't. I wasn't going to grovel and God doesn't do deals.

I tried yet again.

Nothing.

I explained to God how let down I felt - I mean, in the great scheme of things, just one small miracle wasn't too much to ask - was it? I mean, *Come on, give me a break here!*

Depressed, I took out one bottle of water, left the bike and started walking. But then I felt it wasn't wise to just leave it on the side of the road in the middle of nowhere so turned back and asked the shop owner if I could push it into their compound. They agreed and opened a metal door for me. I pushed the bike through.

Just as I was turning to make my way out and begin the long walk into the gloom of late dusk, into the desert in the vague direction of our camp, I thought, *What the Hell - give it one more try.*

I did and she fired up as if there had never been a problem.

(I'm sure I heard a voice in my head saying, "Just testing ...")

Filled with an intense joy, I shoved the bottle of water into my pannier with my left hand (keeping the revs up just in case) and set off across the desert towards our camp. Ten minutes later I had arrived and presented Gareth with an abundance of icy water. The potatoes were cooked, the tin of sweet corn opened and supper was ready. The fire had died down to a glow of coals and we had as much fluid as we wanted to drink, ice cold.

I slept that night under a sky intensely black and bright with stars, watching satellites weave their way across until they disappeared beyond the horizon, emphasising my miniscule insignificance in this immense universe, being very aware of my son sleeping in his tent a few metres away and my wife, daughter and granddaughter snug in their beds somewhere beyond the curvature of the earth.

Tomorrow is our wedding anniversary.

Forty years.

We've done pretty well, all things considered. We made two great kids, young adults now, of course.

That must count for something...

A brief digression on wives (well, my wife)

As I'm spending our 40th wedding anniversary having a jolly while my wife waits for me at home, it's perhaps appropriate to reflect a little.

I'm fortunate in having an understanding wife who knows (although, in all honesty, she does not understand) my periodic need to get away somewhere remote on my bike. To be brutally honest, she hates motorbikes and seems to take an instant and visceral dislike to any bikers who have the audacity to filter past her when she's in a car.

(Perhaps "loathe" would express her feelings more correctly.)

"Another biker trying to kill himself," she will mutter, anger rising at the sheer cheek of anyone being able to escape the hot clutches of a traffic jam in which she is trapped.

In our dotage, we have settled on a mutually tolerant understanding: I will make one month-long bike trip a year until I die or can't ride any more; she will keep a legion of dogs and cats. She doesn't like motorbikes or me riding them; I don't like her animals peeing in the house.

(I understand psychologists with an alphabet of letters after their names call it "Give and Take" or something sounding similarly impressive.)

To be honest, it wasn't a: *Let's sit down and discuss my needs*, sort of thing. I need to get an annual inoculation of the wild outdoors on my bike to keep me living rather than existing. Fortunately she accepts that. I think she knows that if I didn't do the trips I would pretty much cease to be *me*.

And I'd be pretty impossible to live with. (*Or more impossible than I already am,* I hear her say.)

I admire spouses who have the courage, the confidence, in their relationship to say to their partners: Yes, go and *do* it... then come back. To deny someone that which gives them fulfilment is to kill off something within them that is alive and vibrant and life-affirming. One member of a relationship can dig their heels in and say *no!* and, as a consequence, have a compliant but spiritually enfeebled spouse - or allow it and, if he comes back, you'll be sharing your life with someone who is more alive, more at peace, more loving.

(I say *he* because it usually is - but it need not be so. Women too need to escape from the gathering of fuel in vacant lots.)

It's a gamble. The widening gyre just might lose its centre. But I believe it's worth the risk in the long run. Too many people reach old age with dead, unfulfilled eyes, eking out their last miserable hours between ready-meals, day-time television and bickering over the washing up.

So, I have a kind of grudging permission to travel from my wife. (Of course, if she *hadn't* given me her "permission" I would probably still have travelled. I think she knows that and is wise enough not to put it to the test.)

So, your understanding and tolerance is much appreciated, my dear wife. Long may your cats thrive.

Abandoned ships in the desert

The morning started inauspiciously when Gareth noticed, as we were eating our handful of muesli for breakfast, the last of our food, that his front tyre was flat. Off came the wheel - again. A large thorn had pierced right through the tyre wall, in between two knobblies.

We fitted the spare tube as the sun rose across the desert, bringing the heat with it then we set off, leaving our camp site by seven and making good time towards Aral.

Within half an hour of setting off we were flagged down by a posse of policemen who wanted to know where we had been, why we had been there and where we were now going. They didn't seem happy. Someone must have reported having seen two strange looking bikers heading off into the desert where nothing exists for the next gazillion kilometres, so obviously something nefarious had to be going on. We managed to convince them of our innocent intentions and they let us go.

Determined to see these elusive beached ships, perhaps because they are a tangible indication of what Russian hubris has done to the place, we set off along yet another moderately poor dirt road that, evidently, led to a ship graveyard some eighty kilometres west of Aral. The road, raised about a metre above the surrounding land on a sort of causeway, headed across what was once the ancient, muddy bed of the sea which, as I rode, I tried to imagine stretching away from us on all sides, blue to the horizon.

According to Gareth's research, the remnants of the fishing fleet that had, eventually, to be abandoned as the sea dried up - despite valiant attempts to keep them afloat by digging deep channels that linked them to the retreating water - were still there in the desert, most in Uzbekistan but others around Aral. I had seen a photograph, many years before, of a ship sitting incongruously in the middle of a desert landscape with no water at all to the horizon. Since seeing that photograph, I have always wanted to see that ship in the flesh.

Well, we were there, in Kazakhstan, and had the opportunity to fulfil that dream. We had tried the day before and failed. Perhaps this day would be more successful.

But sadly, as so often happens with dreams or with the images one carries in one's head, when reality comes crashing in with soiled boots, the pictures of the mind are so often more real than the reality.

And so it was with the ships.

We rode the eighty long kilometres across this straight, stony track, slewed our way through an area of soft sand and, eventually, came across a poor remnant of what we were looking for.

This was so disappointing. We had spent two days looking for this ship graveyard, riding across hundreds of kilometres of bad roads and sand in an attempt to find them. And after all that time and effort, all that we found were the rusted remains of the internal structure of a single ship, an L-shaped metal frame that didn't even look like a ship, all the outer plates having been removed and, by the look of it, most of the internal plates as well, stripped out and scavenged by local people in much the same way that stones from the walls of abandoned castles were scavenged by contiguous people long ago for building their houses. And in a way, I suppose we were naïve to think that ships left stranded on a desert surface would still be unchanged thirty years later.

We got off our bikes feeling the desert heat beat down on us from above and radiate up at us from the sand below. Beer bottles littered the scene; the stinking carcass of a dead foal fouled the air. White, Banksy-like paintings gave the rusting metal surfaces a surreal quality: here a man in the garb of a sailor urinated against the wall, his expression just a little disapproving as he glanced around to see us watching him; a group of men lolled about, drinking; a man, smoking a cigarette, sat on an oil barrel. The men all had hard faces. None of them was working - a pictorial comment, perhaps, on the loss of jobs in this place when the water left them all behind.

We had hoped to see a ship, some ships, stranded on the dried-up Aral Sea bed, ships that held still the smell of the fish they used to catch. I had imagined us climbing aboard and looking for a souvenir, exploring below decks, the engine room, the bridge. Somehow we expected time to have stood still for thirty years...

Well, you only know when you know.

We turned the bikes round and started on the long trek back to the town of Aral and the main road, but only after I had dropped my bike again while trying to get through a long stretch of soft sand. It had begun to snake about in the wheel ruts, the heavy load pulled me over and I ended up with my front wheel on the outer edge, one leg holding the entire weight of the bike and luggage in the rut and I just couldn't hold it. I let the bike fall and, because it was lying tank down in the sunken tracks, I'm ashamed to say that I just couldn't lift it. I could have removed some of my baggage and got it up but, hot and exhausted, I felt it was easier just to wait for Gareth to back track and give me a hand - which he did a few minutes later.

By late morning we had reached Aral yet again and, after having spent nearly two days looking for the abandoned ships, we turned north heading for the next town, Aqtobe, a mere 580ks away.

Whether it was because I was already tired, having set off at seven that morning, whether it was the heat, I'm not sure, but the desolation of the Steppe got to me during that long ride throughout the afternoon.

A frightful desolation.

A Sodom and Gomorrah of a landscape.

Before, when I commented on the barren emptiness of this vast land that is Kazakhstan, there were at least a few camels and horses and sheep about. At first the camels were a novelty and we wanted to stop and take photos. But then they became like goats, a ubiquitous part of the landscape, ignored unless they fell over (which two did, shambling away from the noise of our bikes, not looking where they were going whilst trying to maintain their dignity). How we laughed!

But today, when we set off after lunch for points north, the next town of any significance was *over five hundred kilometres* away. We filled up our tanks and all our containers, the temperature hovering at just below 40°C.

During the first one hundred and forty kilometres we saw nothing alive except for the occasional bird of prey. Even the telephone poles and rail lines had abandoned us. A desolate and forbidding place. A flat, scrubby landscape where not even grass can live. Occasionally we came across a bare hill of forbidding, grey sand.

There is something scary about this landscape. Maybe it was the heat or the relentlessly cloudless sky or the lack of grass, the bare earth showing through, the total lack of visible animal life.

After two hundred kilometres we came across a wood and iron shack on the side of the road and pulled over to see whether we could get fuel. Broken cars and what was left of a truck littered the ground behind the shack. A toothless old man appeared and we asked him whether he had fuel.

He shook his head.

Could he serve us some *chai?*

He nodded and disappeared inside while Gareth and I divested ourselves of our riding gear and rested in the shade.

While we drank our tea, some men attempted to push-start a 4X4.

After a short break, we rode on into the afternoon...

Strangely, at about 3pm the land changed. It was as if we had entered another country. Sodom had been left behind.

Whether it was the clouds that softened the harsh glare of the sun, the rows of trees that had been planted along each side of the road and which cut off one's vision of the Steppe, flat and featureless, continuing for eternity, I'm not sure; but, in addition to these, the main change was grass. Suddenly the barren ground was covered with a thin layer of short, yellow-green grass as far as the eye could see. Sand ridges became grassy undulations; the raw desert was covered with a veneer of life and lost its threat; animals could be seen grazing; we saw our first tractor since entering Kazakhstan five days before. Even the high-tension electricity cables on wooden poles, like shy girls at a party, returned and quietly dipped their loose wires across the yellow-green landscape.

This was how I always imagined the Steppes: millions of acres of grassland grazed by millions of sheep and horses and goats and cows, an abundant and fertile land. How little did I realise just how tenuous was this inchoate skin of life that covered the barrenness of desert that is Khazakhstan and just how much of it has already been lost.

Getting increasingly tired as the afternoon turned to evening, we tried to find accommodation but without success. A truck-stop motel was full - try thirty kilometres down the road, they suggested, but we knew it was probably going to be a hundred, the next town.

The thirty kilometres came and went - nothing.

Another hundred it would be then. I put my head down and continued riding.

Finally, at 6.30, we arrived at the town of Khromatai and pulled in to a hotel. The receptionist was rude and unhelpful. When we walked in she was on the telephone and, blanking us completely, she continued speaking for the next ten minutes on what seemed to be a social call. Then she muttered about papers, documents, speaking rapid, loud Russian despite knowing we couldn't understand. Gareth wondered whether we hadn't strayed into a restricted area once again and were about to be arrested - like in Russia a few years before.

In the end, we gave up and left.

The next hotel was full but a helpful lady gave us directions to a small, family-run guest-house where we were made welcome. It was after seven. We had been on the road for thirteen hours and were dirty, stinking and exhausted. Too much... too long... too hot.

But the beer was cold and the shower clean, and that made all the difference.

640ks and a childish interlude

Business as usual - today we rode six hundred and forty kilometres across flat, almost featureless Steppe.

The bikes are going well...

SCHOOL REPORT - MY HOLIDAY

This was my holiday.

We saw lots of grass. Mostly yellow grass.

Why is it called a Steppe when it's so flat? Ha ha!

I killed a grouse today. It flew into me. We didn't stop to get it because we weren't camping.

There were no rocks. It was very flat. The road was very good. Up and down a lot but not rattley. It was mostly grassy and not deserty.

I saw lots of kestrels. But they might have been hawks.

Or eagles.

We went fast.

Two policemen in a car stopped us with their flashing light but all they did was ask Gareth how fast his KTM could go. They didn't ask me how fast my bike could go. They liked Gareth's bike more than they like my bike.

They looked at it a long time. I think they stopped us just so they could see it. Then they said we could go.

There were lots of clouds so the sun wasn't shining and it was still hot but not so hot as when the sun is shining. (The sun IS shining but it's above the clouds. So we can't see it.)

In the afternoon I nearly fell asleep a few times so we had to stop at a garage to get something to eat to wake me up. That's because it was so flat and the road was so straight and it was hot and I was tired. I was very tired. That's because we didn't have a single rest for a whole month. In the shop they sell cigarettes so cheap even I can buy them with my pocket money. But I won't. They have pictures of dead people and yucchy people on them so bad it wants to make me sick - much worse than in England.

I'm never going to smoke.

That was my holiday.

Thank you.

These six long days crossing the Kazakhstan Steppe are driving me bloody crazy!

Russia tomorrow - *insha'Allah*.

Three old men

We were thrown out of our hotel room rather abruptly at 7am, not having realised that our cheap deal required us to vacate the room at that time. (Gareth had had a reminder phone call at 6.30 but it was in Russian...)

So we loaded our bikes in the rain for the first time on the trip and headed for the Russian border, through which we passed shortly thereafter surprisingly easily. While we were waiting at customs, we watched as a yellow-eyed border guard coldly intimidated a group of dark-skinned Kazakhs, forcing them with small flicks of one finger to open their pathetic collection of bags for inspection, pull out all their belongings and lay them on the wet ground, expressionless while they crouched in front of him, the picture of servility.

Suddenly, without conscious thought, I had an image of these crouching, intimidated men with ragged holes blown in their heads. There was a reptilian coldness, a ruthlessness in the eyes of their tormentor that might have been entirely a product of my own mind - but it was *there*. I can understand why, during the latter part of WW2, Germans on the eastern front were making desperate attempts to be captured by advancing American troops rather than the Russians.

We left the border and entered Russia, the road lumpy, bruised and battered by time and over use. Over the next few hours we passed through many small towns, people living in the same old, sad, tasteless boxes of apartments with rusted reinforcing exposed through the chipped concrete, although in the smaller villages many still lived in quaint log-built houses.

It has always interested me how the land of two contiguous nations, land that was, for millennia, essentially the same, can, after two countries have arbitrarily drawn a line on a map declaring that, as of now, *this* will be called "Kazakhstan" and *this* "Russia" can become so strikingly different; how, over time, that identical land can be moulded to such an extent by human intervention - planting or cutting down trees, nurturing or poisoning the land, encouraging human settlement or not, fertilizing or denuding the soil - that it takes on a distinctive character all of its own.

As we crossed the Kazakh border into Russia, things changed: where once there was Steppe, now this was gone; the flat land we had been crossing for six days became hilly, covered with trees and cultivated. In Kazakhstan I always felt that it was the land that dominated man, causing him to feel helpless and puny, a trespasser; now, in Russia, it was clear that man had taken hold of the land and dominated it. Fields of startlingly bright sunflowers splashed colour across the horizon; wheat, yellow and ready, waited in neat fields for the harvesters; maize grew tall and green and hay was being gathered into stacks. There is a religious moulding too: Kazakhstan is essentially a Muslim country and that is reflected in the architecture whereas, in Russia, the golden onion domes of orthodox churches are to be seen rising above the roofs of houses in every town.

We stopped early to give the bikes a thorough check-over. Gareth's front sprocket was badly worn and his chain on the point of dying; his front forks had leaked out all their oil. Other than that, both bikes are essentially sound, although mine looks pretty battered and sounds like a tractor with a massive hole in the exhaust. All our tyres are badly worn, the rear probably illegal but the knobbles are still visible so we should be able to make it home. They've lasted longer than we thought they would.

In our cheap hotel we met three Russian men - all called Vladimir, as it turned out - who were well into the vodka. They were endearingly friendly, as most drunk Russian men are, and insisted we join them, sloshing generous dollops of vodka into glasses for Gareth and me, pointing to the label and laughing. A woman called Aliona, who spoke good English, explained the joke: they were drinking a brand of vodka called "Three Old Men"!

Clearly proud of what Russia was doing in Ukraine, they insisted that Putin was a "good president" and that he had made the Americans look like headless chickens - one made chicken noises and flapped his arms like wings to illustrate the point. When learning of our intended route home, they warned us not to go into Ukraine - *"Boom! Boom! Boom!"*

Aliona joined us and noticed my A4 sheets of Russian words and phrases that I was studying and which, I am sad to say, she found rather amusing. Gareth, who is picking up the Cyrillic alphabet quite well now, got into conversation with her about Russian pronunciation and spelling. After a while she left us, to return a few minutes later with a child's First Vocabulary Book which she gave to Gareth as a gift, something I know he treasures.

As evening approached, one of the three old men became increasingly drunk. The other two had left. The drunker he got, the louder he spoke and the more, in his befuddled state, he seemed to think we could understand the Russian he was speaking. Gareth maintained a polite reserve, nodding and making eye contact. I chose an appropriate moment to escape and set off to explore the small town, coming across a herd of cattle being led home from a day in the fields by two men on horseback. I decided to follow them into the lanes and back streets, watching the cows, one by one and in small groups, detach themselves from the herd without prompting and take themselves home to be milked.

Outside the front gates of their houses old women sat on low stools, absorbing the last rays of the setting sun; children played in the street; dogs barked listlessly; a flock of ducklings clustered around their dam in the long grass; apple trees drooped, heavy with fruit, in back yards; flowers had been planted everywhere - in old car tyres, window boxes, even in the opened bonnet of a wrecked car.

Emerging from the back streets onto the main road, I saw a number of middle-aged women standing on the pavement holding up signs advertising rooms to passing truckers. It was clear that poverty had forced them to this expedient in order to raise extra income.

Most houses were constructed from wood or lath and daub, straw showing through the flaking mud plaster, corrugated asbestos roofs, painted shutters hanging askew. Yet, although simply built, each house had been lovingly decorated in some small way, personal touches like patches of decorative brickwork, carved wooden lintels above the windows, carved filigree fascia boards, carefully tended flower and vegetable gardens. The dirt roads between the houses were vibrant with communal life - people of all ages, farm and domestic animals - it could have been a scene from a rural English village before the industrial revolution.

This is the other Russia so often hidden behind the brashness of concrete, the Russia of simple people going about their daily lives, a people with whom we have come into contact occasionally on our travels - too seldom, really, because we pass them by in our mad rush to cover the vast distances of these countries in the limited time we have. And it is only when one takes time to pause, walk behind the street façade and meet the ordinary citizens leading every-day lives that one comes close to touching it again.

A diatribe on a certain type of Russian woman

Nowhere in the world have I encountered a species so rude as a certain type of aggressive Russian woman. This breed has so perfected the attitude of contempt that it has become a lifestyle. If it were an Olympic sport, no one in the world could touch them - gold every time.

Now for the vast majority of Russians, I have nothing but liking and respect; except for this particular species, they are friendly, polite and welcoming - especially when sharing *wodka* is concerned, which seems to be most of the time. Drink with them and you are friends for life, brothers eternally bonded by some obscure Russian law. Older women, mostly, are shy and keep their distance, glancing at us surreptitiously from the corners of their eyes and blushing when caught. But the men walk up to us, engage us in conversation, shake us by the hand, welcome us warmly and genuinely, wish us a safe journey, express pleasure in seeing Gareth and me travelling together.

But the Russian woman I am describing here is something else entirely. Usually in her early fifties, always overweight; heavy brows, lipsticked mouth like a bear trap, permanently turned down at the edges; eyes that bore through you looking for signs of weakness or sin that can be exploited, eyes that deliberately look past you, close enough to let you know that you have been seen but sufficiently blank to demonstrate your total lack of significance to her life or job. If she is on the telephone, she will continue talking for however long she feels like, not giving the slightest indication - a tiny smile or a raised eyebrow or finger - that she recognises your presence and is aware that your time is being wasted. When finished doing whatever it was that so absorbed her, she will not apologise; she will ignore you a little longer, perhaps jot something down on a piece of paper or look something up in a book, just to further underline your insignificance, then pierce you with gimlet eyes and down-turned mouth, waiting, blank-faced.

When you state - in faltering Russian or apologetic English - your needs, she will launch into an aggressive diatribe in rapid-fire Russian, making no allowance at all for the fact that you quite obviously don't understand a word she is saying.

Making "I don't understand" gestures infuriates her and she shouts in your face, repeating what she has just said, punctuating her attack this time with aggressive hand gestures, usually directed at some document, liberally decorated with official stamps, with large letters saying *"NYET!"*

When confronted with a woman like this I can quite easily imagine her in a uniform, cattle prod in one hand, bared electric wires inches from your scrotum in the other, screaming, *"You pay! You pay now!"*

The Russian paranoia became apparent the moment we crossed the border. When thinking of buying a cool drink or ice cream, you discover that the fridge or freezer is locked and you have to ask the shop attendant to come and unlock it so you can choose something to buy - under her watchful eye, of course, just in case you are tempted to steal one.

Bless them! It costs so little to be friendly.

What occasioned this little rant is that, since entering Russia, we have met at least one female, ex-Gulag guard every day after being blessed with a bully-free existence throughout the 'Stans for the past twenty four days. This morning we had the temerity to ask for a cup of coffee with milk, please.

"Nyet moloko," was the blunt and unsmiling reply. But we'd just seen a man drinking what was clearly white coffee a few minutes before at a table just a metre away from us.

So we asked again.

"Nyet."

We were served black coffee. (This is Russia, you fool - drink what's put in front of you and like it or we *keell* you.)

Now it just so happened that I'd seen a fridge in the passage so I took my life in my hands, got up and had a look in it (amazingly, it wasn't locked): milk, one carton and one bottle, both unopened. I knew it was milk because it had a cow on it with distended udder and it said 4%.

I took both out, placed them conspicuously on our table and, when the dear lady caught our eye and saw the milk, both Gareth and I grinned like pantomime twins and stuck our thumbs in the air. We were graced with the minutest up-turn of the corners of her mouth which we considered a victory and cheered, much to the perplexity of the other guests in the dining room. (Gareth and I tend to play games when confronted with this kind of woman, challenging each other to make them smile. We seldom succeed but it helps pass the time and takes the sting out of the insults.)

She quickly suppressed her smile, stomped over to a cupboard somewhere and returned, back ramrod straight to indicate that we were seriously imposing on her patience and good nature by asking for milk in such a frivolous fashion, with two sachets of Nestlé's coffee with creamer and poured them into our cups.

It's called "service" in Russia.

(As an aside: While I was typing this, there was a snippet on the radio about the 20th anniversary of McDonalds' opening in Moscow. The commentator said that, at the time of its opening, Muscovites were bowled over by the fact that the staff smiled when they served them because, in Russia, waitresses don't smile!)

We continued heading west, steadily and doggedly, along an execrable road, much bloodied by hard usage over the years. The surface had been broken, squashed, squeezed and repaired, and then repaired again, until it was no longer clear what was the original road and what the repair. We bumped and bashed our way, always heading west, for eight long hours, overtaking trucks by the hundred going the same way.

But, despite its imperfections, the road was interesting, full of character, craggy and weather-beaten like the face of an old person who has lived long and hard. And it kept us engaged trying to find the least bumpy parts. Let's be honest: it should have been retired years ago, dug up and re-laid, but it suffered from one major draw-back: all the most important roads for thousands of miles around Moscow head, like the spokes of a wheel, in towards the hub - Moscow. We were running against the grain, as it were, not doing what was expected therefore not worth much; for the road, not worth replacing.

We continued travelling through a sparsely populated landscape of wild flower meadows and trees, of scrubby untended ground rich in unused potential, through small farming villages, past old women selling berries on the side of the road. The soil, when tilled, was dark brown and smelt of loam, the crops of wheat and sunflowers abundant. Gareth commented during a break that this vast and mostly unexploited land could, if developed properly, feed the entire world. This is not a manicured or sophisticated land; it is rough at the edges, wild and mostly untamed but so unlike the scary nothingness, the dead Sodom and Gomorrah land of the desert Steppes of Kazakhstan; this land is rich and crying out for development. There is space here for a million people to live and farm and become fat with abundant life.

Why does half the world want to come and live in Britain? Russia could take all the waifs and strays of the world, settle them happily in places like this and hardly notice it.

Later we passed the town of Marx with the great man's statue brooding over its entrance; shortly into the afternoon we crossed the great Volga River, bright blue and two to three miles wide. Everything in this country is done on an epic scale - even the rivers.

We bumped and jolted our way into the afternoon, cirrus clouds striating a pale sky, the temperature cool and pleasant. But our kidneys felt as if they had been out on a Friday night binge and got a kicking from a gang of yobs. They - our kidneys, not the yobs - were asking if they could please pack up now and go home. I didn't enquire what the bikes' suspensions felt like; I was afraid to ask.

I think I have developed Vibration White Finger in my right hand. My brain feels mushy.

After a good five hundred and sixty kilometres under the belt, we stopped at a small, unassuming hotel on the side of the road, looking almost like a run-down house trying to make a little extra on the side; but, once inside, we found it a most pleasant establishment run by two young women, grape vines over the lintel and a pleasant, homely atmosphere.

Which is which?

In the dining room the next morning two men ate their breakfast opposite us: a dark-skinned, dark-haired, dark-eyed Azerbaijani and a light-skinned, blond, blue-eyed Russian. While we watched, they ripped bits of meat off a large hunk of mutton and chased it with beer and a bottle of vodka - as one does.

In Russia...

The fumes coming from where they were sitting made my eyes sting.

The Russian man, in his early thirties, engaged us in conversation (perfectly natural when you're Russian and half drunk), commenting on the World Cup. He felt Germany would win although he conceded that Argentina were good. They discussed our trip although we couldn't understand a word they were saying. The alcohol translated our conversation for them but, sadly, not for us...

Now this is your Task for the Day, Dear Reader:

Two men are sitting at a breakfast table, eating.

One has cornflakes and a cup of tea; the other gnaws on the leg of a sheep and slurps vodka.

One is English, the other Russian.

Which is which?

Answers on a postcard.

Once we had extracted ourselves from the drunken enquiries of our new friends (and to make sure we got on the road before they did), it was another long day heading steadily west, the road worn but good, the land becoming increasingly cultivated as we neared the border with Ukraine but still sparsely populated, the occasional field of ripening wheat and the startling yellow of sunflower fields alternating with wide stretches of trees and wild flower meadows allowed to flourish without interference.

At some time during the day we became swallowed up in the city of Voronezh because we had minimal GPS data for Russia and had to rely on just pointing our front wheels west until we found our way out. Asking the many truck drivers on the roads helped and they pointed us in the right direction.

We had decided to camp just for a change so, on the outskirts of Kursk we stopped to fill up with petrol and buy some tomatoes, pickles, bread and salami then headed out of town where we found a pleasant spot to one side of a field of young wheat and erected our tents.

It decided to choose this night, though, to rain. Hard.

A great bitterness

The deluge lasted all night and both our tents leaked a little so it was a damp and disgruntled pair that packed up in a brief dry spell the next morning. Fortunately we had decided not to camp further into the fields where we had reconnoitred the evening before, because a *very* steep ravine would have stood between us and the road and we would have been faced with a long wait until the ground had dried or find a route round because the claggy mud of the track, even when flat, was almost impossible to ride along. Gareth dropped his bike and this glutinous mud began to pack inside his front mudguard - as it had done in Morocco - and jam the wheel.

But after a great deal of sliding and struggling, with the laden bikes just wanting to lie down in the mud, we made it to the road and headed for the border.

This last one hundred miles of western Russia bordering Ukraine is quite beautiful in a wild, unkempt, unspoilt way. It doesn't have the grand high mountains or the prettiness of chocolate box countryside, but it's a ragged, rough-and-ready land that I love riding through. The villages through which we passed were obviously poor - there were no towns of note - and residents supplemented their incomes by keeping ducks and chickens, a cow or a goat or sheep, all of which were either tethered or allowed to roam freely and scratch about in the grassy land between their front picket fences and the road, a swathe of about twenty metres on either side that seems to be deliberately left for this purpose. No water is piped to the small, crudely-built houses and, at intervals along the road reserve were wells, each covered with a quaint, pitched little roof.

An image that stuck in my mind, as these random flashes of life sometimes do as one speeds along through the countryside, is this: at one of the wells a dark-haired young woman in a blouse and long skirt was winding up the water bucket whilst, in the lush grass behind her a mother duck and her ducklings waddled in muddy contentment. (I could almost hear someone singing a twee folk song whilst doves frolicked in the air above her head. I'm sure she was dark-eyed and bare-foot but I was past her before I could notice these other details.)

It was sad to think though, that amongst this bucolic serenity, just a short distance away, people were fighting and being killed over a piece of disputed territory.

As we approached the border with Ukraine, I kept my eye open for signs of the conflict but there were none. Gareth was disappointed to have missed the opportunity of pasting an *Eat My Dirt* sticker on a Russian tank and photographing it to help promote sales. (Or, maybe, fortunately!)

Other than being shouted at by an irascible Russian border official who took exception to my riding through an open barrier without written permission (with official stamps attached), we passed through to the Ukrainian side without problems. We noticed a few small, token gestures of resistance to any potential threat from Russian dissidents - some sand-bagged strong-points, unmanned, that might have kept a determined foe at bay for about - well, five minutes.

Sadly, the first border guard we met on Ukrainian soil attempted to solicit a bribe, withholding our documents and attempting, in very poor English, to convey to us that he wanted money. We just acted ignorant, as we usually do in these situations, and waited him out. In the end, he managed to find the word he wanted: "tradition". He claimed it was *a tradition* for guards to be paid some money when you passed through.

We just laughed, took our passports out of his hand and said, "Not a tradition in the UK, mate!"

(We only came to understand the significance this term later and its effect on Ukrainian society.)

I must admit I was saddened by this undignified solicitation. In the Russia-Ukraine conflict, I have always felt that the Ukrainians hold the moral high ground and that Putin, the kleptocrat - with his dubious disclaimers that he is in any way supporting the dissidents - is the rogue in this tragedy. As a consequence, I found it disappointing that one cringing, small-minded man could be allowed to taint a visitor's perception of an entire country - because it *does*. The officials at a border are the first representatives of a state that one meets and one, rightly or wrongly, makes an initial judgement about the entire country based on these officials. And usually it's a valid judgement. Sloppy, lazy officials, eating food while they process your entry or dealing with you in a rude, dismissive manner reveal much about the country they represent. Bent officials who attempt to solicit bribes imply a country that winks at corruption. Border officials who interact with you whilst reclining on a bed and watching soaps on a conveniently placed telly, taking an hour to complete one application form, leads one to make certain assumptions about the productivity and work ethic of that country.

Anyway, once through customs (after photos with smiling border guards, guns and all) we followed a shockingly bad road for twenty kilometres or so until we joined the main east-west road to Kiev. After all the warnings, the *Boom! Boom!* threats we've had from so many people (especially my wife), crossing into Ukraine was something of an anti-climax. This does not, of course, detract from the tragedy of what is happening further south.

During the mid-afternoon the whole world turned dark and, for about half an hour, we rode through a Noah's flood of a cloudburst. But eventually the storm passed and we made good time for a number of hours until we reached the impressive city of Kiev just after four. At the entrance to the city and on either side of the main bridge were sand-bag gun emplacements but these too were unmanned so obviously no trouble was expected.

It took us over an hour to cross the city, beautiful in its setting around the wide Dnieper River, the vast, stainless steel, sixty-two metre high Motherland Statue dominating the city skyline while the golden domes of Orthodox churches flashed in the late evening sunlight.

We passed through Kiev quite quickly and it makes me feel guilty that I have seemed to dismiss this capital city so casually, especially as the war between troops loyal to the government and pro-Russian separatists being fought in the Donetsk and Luhansk region has been central to much of our planning for our return journey.

This country, Ukraine, and, more particularly its capital, Kiev, deserve some degree of peace and stability after their traumatic recent past history. In the brief time we were there it became clear just what a divided country it is and why the fighting further south is so bitter.

During its time as part of the Soviet Union, Russia adopted a deliberate policy of so-called "Russification" of Ukraine and especially Kiev. Whole-scale Russian migration into Ukraine was encouraged to the extent that, now, in the twenty-first century, this country is part Russian, part Ukrainian. Half of their language is made up of Russian vocabulary; many Ukrainians have family members who are Russian and who live in Russia; 80% of the people living in the disputed south eastern border lands would regard themselves as Russian even though they carry Ukrainian passports. So, with independence in 1991 and the aftermath of the Orange Revolution, the country has suffered a crisis of identity: are they Russian or Ukrainian? Are they going to align themselves with the Russian or European sphere of influence?

For those wanting closer ties with Russia, these are important questions, important enough to take up arms. And Moscow has grown tired of its steady loss of influence, of power, as the Soviet Union collapsed and, one by one, its erstwhile satellite states turned west and joined the European Union.

And there is great bitterness deep down. Even as far back as the 17th century, Ukraine was beginning to fall under the Russian mantle. After having been subsumed into the vast Soviet state by becoming one of the founding republics of the Soviet Union in 1922, Ukrainians gradually lost autonomy and, with it, their sense of identity as a nation. Kiev became totally dominated by Russians who controlled the country's administration; ethnic Ukrainians were pushed to the outskirts and treated as lower class citizens.

In 1917, during the Russian Revolution, Kiev briefly became the capital of a short-lived Ukrainian state before being caught in the middle of WW1, occupied by the Germans, then involved in the Russian Civil and the Polish-Russian Wars, changing hands *sixteen times* in two years.

After WW1 Kiev gradually restored itself as the centre of Ukrainian life as Russian influence waned, but then came the Great Famine of 1932-33 and Stalin's Great Purge in 1937-38 when most of the city's intelligentsia were eliminated.

The famine and purges alone will help us understand the depth of feeling in those Ukrainians who oppose Russian influence/interference today.

"The 1932-33 famine (*Golodomor* - literally, murder by starvation) caused 5-7 million deaths, most in Ukraine after their resistance to collectivisation. 'A carefully organised mass crime intended to destroy Ukrainian national aspirations' wrote leading Ukrainian historian, Stanislav Kulchytsky.

"The famine, by some estimates, destroyed about a sixth of the population of Ukraine. It killed indiscriminately. No category of the population was spared, and survival in the affected areas depended not on personal traits but on skill in hiding food, twists of fate and cannibalism. Death was so pervasive, gruesome, and indiscriminate, and it affected Ukrainians so disproportionately, that what took place can justly be described as genocide..." (excerpts from David Slater's book: *"It Was a Long Time Ago, and it Never Happened Anyway"* .)

The turmoil in the life of the city continued during WW2 when Kiev was occupied by German troops for just over two years. More than 600,000 Soviet soldiers were killed or captured during the Battle of Kiev in 1941. Just before they were finally pushed out, Russian soldiers dynamited most of the buildings in the city centre leaving 25,000 people homeless. Allegedly, in an act of reprisal, the Germans rounded up all the local Jews and, over the course of 29-30 September 1941, massacred nearly 34,000 of them at Babi Yar.

But, once again, Kiev recovered after the war to become the third most important city in the Soviet Union. And then came the Chernobyl Nuclear Power Plant disaster in 1986, just a hundred kilometres north of the city.

Finally, with the dissolution of the Soviet Union, Ukraine declared its independence on 24 August 1991 and the struggle to create a Ukrainian state, free from Russian influence, began. Sadly the massive corruption and vote rigging that led to the Orange Revolution has still not been eliminated from Ukrainian society as it lurches towards re-discovering its identity.

It's a city, a country, so rich in history and culture, so blood-soaked in its genesis, that the continued conflict with Russian separatists in the south makes one's heart bleed. Both Gareth and I felt we would love to visit again and spend more time there, treat it with more respect than just another country to ride across on our way home.

Once through Kiev, we stopped for the night at a small but delightful hotel. Everything worked. It even had toilet paper - *Whoooo!* The tiles weren't cracked and water didn't leak from the cistern. The beer was cold. All is forgiven.

There was a style and precision about everything; the build quality was excellent, such a change after having travelled through Soviet and ex-Soviet countries for so long. We were looked after by a waitress/hostess so cute and endearing I wanted to ask her if she'd like to be my daughter. What a contrast to the dead-eyed surliness we so often have had to endure over the past weeks, lobotomised automatons to whom any idea of service is as foreign as the thought that guests staying in a hotel room just *might* enjoy a few squares of toilet paper and a bath plug, or a bathroom that won't kill them with flesh-eating germs or live electricity from poorly-insulated appliances. (Sorry - I detect a shrillness creeping into in my voice again.)

My otherwise reliable old KLE had, over the past few days, made its mind up that it had the right to decide, in a purely arbitrary manner, whether it wanted to start or not. (You remember, it first occurred when I was buying water for our desert camp.)

This I found somewhat annoying, as you can imagine, especially as, whenever this happened, Gareth had to tow me to get the engine going again and I would end up sliding all over the road with a locked back wheel before the engine finally turned over. And even then it was a lottery whether it would start. Being towed on a bike is a somewhat perilous act, as those of you who have tried it will testify. One's normal ability to lean into a turn is denied by the pull of the bike in front and, get the tow line crooked at any stage and it will want to drag you over.

That evening, in the town of Lutsk where we were spending the night, I suffered the indignity of being towed for three kilometres through rush-hour traffic, after sliding and snaking along, back wheel refusing to turn, with the big KTM dragging me along like a reluctant child - and nothing would make it start.

Yet, later, after pushing it to the parking lot at the back of the hotel for the night, I thought I'd give it a quick jab on the starter and, sweet as a kitten, it instantly recovered from its prolonged sulk and started.

Gareth thinks it might be the plugs that have carboned up after so many miles of high altitude.

Very frustrating.

Bribery in Ukraine

To be honest, I was sad.

Perhaps "disappointed" would be a preferable word.

This feeling was brought about by a long conversation we had with the Youth Pastor of the church we were visiting in Lutsk for the day. Ukrainian born, intelligent, educated and well-spoken, he informed us, with sadness and disappointment clouding his face, that his country is endemically and institutionally corrupt, from the bottom to the very top. *Everything* is paid for; everything has its price.

"That's how life works here," he told us with a resigned smile.

You pay to be appointed to a job - like a border official - and then you collect money from people passing through to cover your initial outlay. A figure of $20,000 for the position of border security guard was mentioned and this, evidently, can be recouped within a year. Payments are passed up the chain, of course, everyone getting their cut, right up to ministerial level.

Now I understood what the border guard who withheld our documents was trying to explain when he was asking for money and referring to his request as a "tradition".

Evidently, police will target successful businesses with a non-existent "problem"; then, on a payment of a "fine", the problem will disappear. Refuse to pay the fine and you will find your business closed down until the "problem" has been sorted out. Even doctors are in on the act. Evidently it is not uncommon for them to deliberately create a delay in the waiting room and then you can jump the queue on payment of a bribe - although, of course, it's not called that. It's a greasing of the wheels of society, the lubricant that keeps everything going. University students will only get good grades if they pay. No payment to the lecturer, no good grades. In fact, he told us, all the students from any class have to club together to raise the required sum before their grades are decided. No student can afford not to contribute.

"But," he added, "in a perverse way, the system *works*. Anything can happen because all it takes is a payment. Whatever problem you have, a payment will make it go away."

It sounded to me for a moment almost as if he was proud of the system, was, in fact, supporting it and I challenged him on this.

He looked sad. "No," he quickly clarified, "it is a bad system and it should be done away with but, at the moment, corruption *is* the system and it is the only way things get done. The only way to purge the country of corruption," he added, "would be for a Hitler or a Stalin to take over and massacre a few million people. That's the only way it would stop because it goes to the very top."

I asked him whether the Mafia existed in Ukraine and he laughed ruefully and said, "The government *is* the Mafia!"

Ukraine is a beautiful country and, as with the 'Stans, you wish them well in their new freedom and independence, you *will* them to succeed, to replace the authoritarian Soviet regime with something more tolerant, enlightened, democratic - but, sadly, it seems that this is not a natural consequence of freedom as much as we would like it to be. Zimbabwe broke free from the so-called yoke of British colonialism and what it got in return was Mugabe. Enough said. South Africa got Zuma after a brief period of enlightenment under Nelson Mandela.

Turkmenistan is still a basket case - bring back the Soviets! Maybe Ukraine needs Putin to kick some sense into its corrupt systems and then start all over again.

Let's be honest, the Soviets weren't - and aren't - all bad, even though I tend to describe them sometimes in somewhat unflattering terms. In Tajikistan the Russians educated rural people - men and women - to a far higher level than contiguous peoples in Afghanistan and China; and Russia's dedication to equality of all soviet citizens, male and female, allowed women in the USSR to rise to positions of influence and power far greater than in many Western countries, where a glass ceiling still exists for many women. And I would certainly support the Soviet system and its treatment of women over many so-called enlightened Arab states, some of whom feel that women ought not to be educated *at all* or even drive a car unless in the presence of a male family member.

Maybe we need a Putin-led autocracy to push some people around and introduce Soviet equality there too.

We'd all love the world to be divided into black and white, the good guys and the bad, those we support and those we oppose; but, sadly, it's never as simple as that. The whole world evolves and mutates and stumbles its way forward - and we make the best of it we can.

The next day, Sunday, was the only rest day that we took on the whole five-week journey. Distances were just too great to afford ourselves that luxury.

After a lively church service conducted in Ukrainian (translated *sotto voce* by a friendly woman who took us under her wing for the duration) we were shown about the Old Town by two young lasses from the youth group, Marina and Solomia, who revelled, I think, in being associated with these two foreigners (especially Gareth) and with whom they could practice their remarkably good English. They were clearly proud of being Ukrainian but they, too, sadly commented on the endemic corruption that permeates every aspect of their society. Even high school students, they insisted, have to collect money to pay their teachers to ensure good grades.

If Ukraine ever hopes to take its place as part of the European Union, something that those leaning towards the West hope might happen one day, they are going to have to eradicate this disease that is blighting their land.

Although we saw very little of Ukraine, passing through on the last days of our trip and eager to get on, I have an ambivalence about the country that needs further investigation. The people are friendly and welcoming and there is clear evidence that a great deal of effort has been, and still is being, put into the infrastructure. It is, however, still a divided and deeply flawed country. Hopefully, as the younger generation - represented so strongly by Marina and Solomia - mature and can begin to influence the nature of their society, things will change.

Poland and home

And so, by late morning the next day, we were in Poland and back in the European Union. At last my insurance kicked in!

As we crossed the border, we both felt an almost palpable change in the atmosphere. Gareth, I think, put his finger on it when he said, "It's the lack of paranoia."

At last one can live under the assumption that authorities trust you to do right and will only investigate you if they have reason to believe otherwise; over the past month, there has been a distinct feeling somewhere in the back of the mind that those in power automatically assume that you are up to no good and consequently need to be watched - guilty until proven innocent instead of the other way round. I know that's a simplistic assessment but the feeling is there.

And so, really, our trip is pretty much over bar the last 1600ks along modern motorways back to the UK. Our knobblies are worn down to the nub and we keep on looking at them, trying to convince ourselves that they are not illegal and will last us until we get home. My bike's annoying intermittent refusal to start crops up occasionally but we can cope. It always starts again after a brief wait.

Sometimes it's just not in the mood.

It's been a hard trip. 12,000ks in five weeks; just the one rest day. I've lost a lot of weight even though I don't have much to lose.

A Polish guy walked up to us at a petrol station and said how good it was to see such dirty bikes. We discussed our trip and he was impressed. As a biker, he said, he's seen too many clean Sunday bikes, polished for a short weekly run on tar so long as the weather is good.

Yes, our bikes look dirty and worn, bungees and wire and zip ties hanging from here and there holding things together, that *ingrained* dirt that comes from weeks on the road. Our bodies are the same - tanned, worn, red-eyed. But despite this, there is a sense of accomplishment that buoys the spirit.

In a few days we will be home. Life will settle down once again to the routine of daily living. But the memories will always remain, jostling aside more mundane things in those times when the mind casts itself back in the still, twilight moments of early dawn or, when you least expect it, taking you back.

Postscript

All experience is knowledge, they say. As you know, I knew almost nothing of the 'Stans before we left.

Now I know just a little.

I know that, if I could have my time again, in an ideal world, I would ride the two-day section from Langar > Shayman > Murghab twice, there and back, just for the hell of it, for the sheer joy of it. Then I'd ride the Bartang Pass from Muzkol to Rushan (which we couldn't do because of Gareth's bike drinking fuel and the landslide which put us on the wrong side of it). Finally, I'd do the track to Lake Song-Kol and sleep the night in the mountains again then continue south to Ak Tal.

There, now I've done all the grunt work for you, all you've got to do is *do it* - it'll be the trip of a lifetime. (If you've got lots of money and can fly your bike in and out of Almaty, you could do all of this in two weeks - so long as there are no landslides!)

And so, to quote Brett Houle just once more, a biker who seems to understand what I have tried to capture in this account of our brief trip into Central Asia:

"Here's to riding more than we wrench. Here's to over the hills and far away. Here's to staying fully alive."

PS - Our GPS track, as well as photographs from the trip, are on Gareth's website, if you're interested: www.hareti.co.uk

PPS - Gareth tells me he's looking for an old bike he can leave in Bishkek. Looks like we're going there again. And again. Central Asia does that to you.

PPPS - (Got to stop this - it's getting silly.) My faithful KLE500 was so trashed by the trip that when I got home I decided to scrap it. But I found an identical bike - same colour, same year. Mine had 100,000ks on the clock; this one, although seven years old, had only done 4,000ks. Almost new.

Here's to the next seven years and 100,000ks - by then I'll be seventy.

Mmmmm - where to next...?

Contact

If you'd like to contact me about anything in this travelogue, feel free to email me on lgbransby@hotmail.com.

If you'd like to read any of my other travelogues or novels, you'll find them on Amazon.

Happy riding... and, hey, let's be careful out there.

Other books by Lawrence Bransby

Travelogues:

A Pass too Far
Travels in Central Asia

Trans-Africa by Motorcycle
A Father's Diary

There are no Fat People in Morocco

By Motorcycle through Vietnam
Reflections on a Gracious People

Plymouth-Dakar Old Bangers Rally

Venture into Russia
Three Motorcycle Journeys

The Wakhan Corridor

A Walk to LorencoMarques
Reminiscences of a 13-year-old

By Bicycle to Beira
Reminiscences of a 15-year-old

Plymouth-Dakar/Banjul Old Bangers Challenge

Adult Novels:

Life-Blood - Earth-Blood

A Matter of Conscience

Second Sailor, Other Son

Teenage Novels

Down Street
Winner of the MER Prize for Youth Literature

Remember the Whales
Winner of the J.P. van Der Walt Prize

A Mountaintop Experience
Book Chat South African Book of the Year 1993

The Geek in Shining Armour
Of Roosters, Dogs and Cardboard Boxes

The Boy who Counted to a Million
Winner of the Sir Percy Fitzpatrick Prize;
MNET Award Finalist '96

Outside the Walls

Printed in Great Britain
by Amazon